NOT GUILTY!
The Script

The Negro National Anthem

Lift every voice and sing
Till earth and heaven ring,
Ring with the harmonies of Liberty;
Let our rejoicing rise
High as the listening skies,
Let it resound loud as the rolling sea.
Sing a song full of the faith that the dark past has taught us,
Sing a song full of the hope that the present has brought us,
Facing the rising sun of our new day begun
Let us march on till victory is won.

So begins the Black National Anthem, written by James Weldon Johnson in 1900. Lift Every Voice is the name of the joint imprint of The Institute for Black Family Development and Moody Press, a division of the Moody Bible Institute.

Our vision is to advance the cause of Christ through publishing African-American Christians who educate, edify, and disciple Christians in the church community through quality books written for African-Americans.

The Institute for Black Family Development is a national Christian organization. It offers degreed and nondegreed training nationally and internationally to established and emerging leaders from churches and Christian organizations. To learn more about The Institute for Black Family Development write us at:

The Institute for Black Family Development
15151 Faust
Detroit, Michigan 48223

NOT GUILTY!
The Script

Written by John P. Kee

Scripture quotations marked NKJV are taken from the *New King James Version*. Copy-
right © 1982 by Thomas Nelson, Inc. Used by permission. All rights reserved.

Scripture quotations marked KJV are taken from the King James Version.

ISBN: 0-8024-1517-2

1 3 5 7 9 10 8 6 4 2

Printed in the United States of America

This book is dedicated to a true warrior gone to take his rest.
James "Mr. Ben" Truesdale
June 13, 1957–July 7, 2001
Eternal Partaker

CONTENTS

INTRODUCTION

As I sat down to record twenty-two years of inner-city ministry, I discovered that it could not all be done in two or three hundred pages. It was simply too much information. While my work as a gospel-music artist has touched the lives of many thousands of people, it occurred to me this time that music may not be enough. As I listened to the twenty-two songs on my double CD *Not Guilty*, I was convinced that I had more to say on the subject.

One night while sitting in my musical chambers, eyes closed, listening with my heart, I saw more than a concept video. I actually saw a movie that dealt with boldness, being accused, taking a stand, being tried, justified, and then acquitted. It was clear from the motion pictures in my mind that the script was inevitable. I dashed to the computer, and this literary composition was birthed.

Many names and events have been altered to protect those who have not yet been informed that they are "not guilty." Although the script, book, and movie may be considered a fictitious, didactic medium of entertainment, there is a deep, profound message of faith and true deliverance in this story. I am sure that just as the CD did, this book will create dialogue for those who are chained, bound, and shackled so that they may understand that they too have been acquitted.

After being set free from the things that had you bound, don't forget that you don't have to ever be enslaved to your past. In life many of us will be faced with turbulent times, but we must understand as Christians that many times it is not what we see, feel, or experience; it is the spirit of the thing, the illusion of darkness. You are **NOT GUILTY!**

1

SATURDAY NIGHT LIVE

It was 8:30 on a Saturday night in early April. I was standing at the garage, preparing for my normal weekend routine. I kissed my family good-bye and headed to the inner city of Charlotte, North Carolina. As crazy as it may sound, that is where I find tranquility, a peace that surpasses all understanding.

The Lord delivered me from a 'hood in Charlotte that, according to local and state crime statistics, was one of the most dangerous places to live. Yet every Saturday night I put on my gear and head to this place called Double Oaks, a neighborhood noted for its gang and drug activity. I go there not as Pastor John P. Kee but as one of the regulars of the area. Many folks question my intentions: "Why would a man of your caliber hang out in a place like this?" Well, it goes back to 1979, '80, and '81. I often testify about that grim period in my life. As I look back now, I realize that I could not have made it out of those years without the hand of the Lord. You name it: pimping, slinging, hustling—they were all a part of my modus operandi. However, breaking down and then restoring lost souls is a part of God's M.O. And that's precisely what He did for me. Consequently, I have gained a deeper appreciation for Romans 5:8—"While we were yet sinners,

Christ died for us" (KJV). So when I speak or sing to people about the power of Jesus Christ in a person's life, it comes from personal experience.

For twenty years I longed to come back to the neighborhood that I had poisoned and deceived when I was "yet a sinner" and do whatever I could to bring healing and restoration. It only stood to reason that street ministry to the hustlers, pimps, and prostitutes would be an integral part of my mission. Looking at the present situation in Double Oaks, I believe in my heart that I have accomplished at least 40 percent of my goal.

In 1997, I purchased close to seven acres of land and started to build my ultimate dream—a multipurpose community center. Operated by our church, New Life Fellowship Center, the facility houses our worship service, a community movie theater, the Night Court Basketball outreach program, and even a Christian nightclub, The Praise Connection. As you can see, when I say "multipurpose," I mean *multi*purpose. The building is home to over fifty programs, and we have been able to give vast amounts of money back to the community with no government assistance.

I surrounded myself with leaders who were sold out to this vision, a vision to go in and take territory from the Enemy. At each church service, as we preached and taught God's Word, the altars overflowed with people. Every time we came together, life-changing experiences could be documented. God had given us a vehicle for ministry that allowed people of all ages to lay down their sins and guilt, without fear of judgment. As a pastor and evangelist, I believed in my heart that the same Word that pricked my spirit and moved me to submit to God could change anybody's life.

And it did. After the opening of the Fellowship Center, we were cramming more than 1,500 people into a 1,100-seat auditorium every week. I saw God turn prostitutes into missionaries and pimps into purveyors of the Gospel. Next to the Fellowship Center we planned to build the Life Center, a larger worship sanctuary. The city had given us eighteen acres of land on the south side of our property, and we were overjoyed. This, of course, could not have made the Enemy happy. Let me explain why.

Seven days prior to the opening of our church, there were two murders in Double Oaks. The neighborhood, it seemed, was the perfect place for crime. The streetlights were outdated and rarely lit. There was an element of darkness—both physical and spiritual—that permeated the area. On the north side of our property stood an acre of trees. While building the fellowship center, I noticed that behind this wooded area, a lot of illegal activity took place. I was a firm believer that much of the bad reputation that Double Oaks had was not created by those who lived there but by people who were not residents of the area. So I did the unthinkable. I pulled together a few of the men of God at our church and cut down all of the trees and undergrowth and cleared the entire area. This enabled us to see all the way over to Newland Road, which borders the north side of our property. Soon enough, the drivers of eighteen-wheelers that once frequented the area on dark nights discovered they no longer had a place to conduct business with local prostitutes. The screeching of their tires as they pulled away signaled their disgust—they knew they had lost one of their best hideaways. The many people who would pull onto our property and hide behind that wooded area to purchase drugs were amazed to find that the light from our church now cast its glow on Newland Road and beyond. I likened it to the light of the Holy Ghost shining throughout this dark neighborhood. There was a new Sheriff in town.

I still had one major concern, though. Double Oaks sits on approximately fifty-two acres, and though we could light up the northern side of the neighborhood, there were still some hidden areas that I wanted to reach.

Twenty years ago I had sold drugs across the street from Double Oaks, in a small convenience store. I operated the store with an ex-girlfriend and her mother. At the time, it was the perfect arrangement. I was able to sell drugs and involve myself in various other areas of illegal mischief, and it was never detected because of my ex-girlfriend's and her mother's good names and reputations in the community. I lived approximately six blocks away on Arden Street, where I bought and exchanged drugs on a daily basis. My reputation was not only with street thugs and those who were labeled no-gooders and lowlifes. I also had a following with preachers and churchgoing people who would stop by my store on a daily basis for a "hook-up"—i.e., a drug purchase. Twenty years after my deliverance from that life, many of those "church-going people" are still skeptical about the veracity of my faith.

God has blessed me in many ways. The fame and the wealth that I have experienced as a gospel-music artist have surpassed that of the average ex-drug dealer. So it does not surprise me when the skeptics say there is no way God could transform a thug into a minister. As a pastor, I strive to teach the people of God to see them as God sees them, not as men do.

That Saturday night, I arrived in Double Oaks at about 9:20. It was already dark and the night was jumping. There were two strip clubs at the top of Statesville Avenue, one at the bottom, and approximately six liquor establishments within a one-mile radius. And there I stood, a man of faith, believing in my heart that I could change the destinies of those who had other agendas.

My first encounter that night was with a prostitute by the name of Big D. I slowed my car down and began to converse with her. Thinking I was a cop, she immediately put up a barrier. I assured her without expressing my true identity that I was not the police. I wanted to encourage her to get off the streets. I invited her to our church. To my surprise she told me that she had already been there.

She bent down, looked into my car, and could not hide her emotions. On her face I saw disgust, shame, and guilt. She was utterly embarrassed. It was as though a veil had been lifted and she was exposed. I assured her that I was not riding out to judge any man or woman. I just wanted to remind her that the Lord loved her. I got out of the car and embraced her. Her immediate concern was that the police officers in the neighborhood knew that she was a prostitute and she did not want me to bring trouble to myself because of this gesture of compassion. I told her that had I been concerned about that kind of thing, I would never have left home.

I prayed with her. When we were finished, she suddenly began to share her story. She had been kicked out of her home at age sixteen. She had four kids who had been taken by the state. She was renting a little room in Double Oaks. She told me she worked just to make ends meet. She looked at me with tears in her eyes and said, "I just want my kids back." I interrupted her and said, "D, you don't owe me or anyone else an explanation for what God is delivering you from." I embraced her again, and she assured me that I would see her in church on Sunday.

I have discovered that many sincere Christians approach street ministry with the wrong attitude. They try to bring about an immediate revival, with no follow-up effort. This is why I love the Double Oaks area. I am able to minister, not only in the four-wall structure of the church service, but out on the streets and alleys of the 'hood.

Next, I encountered a young man for whom I had been praying for nearly a decade. His name is Duey Wright, a.k.a. "Do-Wright." Do-Wright, at thirty-seven, was a couple of years younger than I. Back in my drug-selling days, he had been a runner—one who transports money and goods between pushers and users. He ran for me for a while, but then he moved up on "the Hill"—the area in Double Oaks where all of the hustlers hung out, located directly across the street from the basketball courts. I was amazed to come back and find Duey still doing the same things we were doing two decades ago. Do-Wright walked with a limp. He had gotten warning shots in his legs at least three times. And believe it or not, he never would do right. He was violating the drug dealer's three rules of conduct:

(1) Don't skim money off the top,
(2) Don't smoke your own stash, and
(3) Make the profit before you spend the proceeds.

He flagged me down and said, "Pastor Kee, let me get $20."

I said, "How can you be a player and be broke?"

He told me he was not a player, he was a pimp, and he had not cashed in yet; the night was still early. I told him I could not give out money. I had stopped buying drugs a long time ago. He assured me it was not for drugs; he was hungry. I told him I would take him up the Hill and buy him something to eat. He jumped in the car, and we drove to Bojangles Restaurant, which served the hottest chicken this side of the Mississippi. I pulled up to the window and let him order. He ordered a ten-piece family pack.

I smiled. "I did not ask you to order for me *and* you."

He said that he did not. "This is for me," he explained.

After he ordered his sides and drink, the total came to $15. He assured me he would pay me back. I told him, "No, I will put it in church for you and put your name on it."

I loved Duey. I stayed on his case all the time about looking into the mirror and making some decisions that could change his condition, so he was accustomed to my evangelistic antics. We drove around and picked up the food, and to my surprise, Duey proceeded to eat every piece of chicken, fries, and rice—like he had not eaten in three weeks. I felt really bad. I had prejudged my brother. I felt that if I had given him money, he would have walked around the block and bought himself some crack. But you should have seen how this man ate that chicken.

"Slow down, cuz," I told him. "You are about to bite your hand."

"I told you I was hungry," he said.

I could not wait another moment. I said, "Do-Wright, I apologize. I prejudged you. When you asked me for $20 to eat, I did not give it to you because I felt like you would go and smoke some crack."

"Don't apologize," he said. "If you had given me that $20, I would have smoked some crack—but thank you for this meal."

We laughed, and I took him home. I knew I had about seven

minutes left with him until he would jump out of the car and I would not see him again until the next day. So, instead of beating up on him, I began to love him. I asked him where he was going.

"I'm headed to the pool hall, but you can let me out here."

"No, I'll drop you off," I told him.

The pool hall was two miles away. With this extra drive time, I began to share my testimony, which allowed Duey to ask me questions about my newfound stability. I could tell that he was not only interested; he truly desired a life change. I believe that once you tap into the knowledge of God, He will open doors that will allow you to commit to Him.

My conversation with Duey became very intense, and it was proving to be my kind of evening. By now, it was a half hour before midnight. There we were at the pool hall. Duey was ready to jump out of the car, but I was not finished. So I had a decision to make: Do I leave him there or hang out with him another hour? As he climbed out of my car, I exited with him.

He looked at me and said, "Where are you goin'?"

"I'm going in the pool hall with you."

"Pastor Kee, you can't go in there."

I knew what he meant. The sign read POOL HALL, but there were many other activities going on in that place. On his face I saw disbelief that I would spend this much time with him. Back in the day, when I was nineteen and he was seventeen, Duey and I were considered "road dogs." Although I was only two years older than he, he now looked several years older than I. The streets had taken a toll on Duey Wright. I could tell in his red eyes that he still respected me. It was not like the days of old when the respect came with a criminal price. But somewhere in my heart, I believed he really knew I had changed and he respected the Spirit of God that dwelled in me.

I made him a deal. I said, "I will play you a game of eight ball. If I win, I pick you up in the morning for church at 11:30. If you win, I won't bug you about coming to church for a month."

"You got a deal," he said with a smile.

As I walked in the pool hall I saw a lot of old acquaintances, some I thought were dead, and others I thought were still locked up. Lenny T was an old hustler who ran the liquor house two blocks from the store where I worked. He had to be pushing 112 years old. Actually, he was seventy-five—but still smooth. He wore double-knit spit-shine pants and a silk shirt with a dog collar from the early '70s. When he saw me, his jaw dropped. "I can't believe that you're in here," he said. I embraced him and we began to talk about old times. Duey interrupted and told me to hurry up so that I could receive my whippin'. *Can you believe it? I thought to myself. The good Pastor Kee is hanging out in the pool hall after 11:00 P.M. What would the church folks say about this?* Please don't be offended, but tagged onto that last thought was this postscript: *Who cares?*

We flipped a coin to see who would break.

One of the young boys looking on made a comment. "Who is this dude that he can walk into the pool room and get a table this fast?"

Almost immediately, I heard an old man by the name of Chop Monk say, "That is John P. Kee, pastor of the church in the 'hood."

I told Duey that I was going to beat him and he could not renege on church service. He assured me that my skills were not what they were twenty years ago. He didn't know that on the bottom floor of my house there was a pool table, and that at least once every two weeks I made sure my game was still intact. He won the toss, broke the racked balls, and dropped small. His next shot was a 3 ball in the corner. He missed. I had a four-ball run and the rest is history. It's called an old-fashioned spanking. He smiled in defeat and promised me that he would be ready at 11:30.

I passed out a few church cards. It was great to see some of the guys, for there is an old myth in the 'hood—if you don't see somebody within 365 days, he is either dead or in jail. One of the guys, "Sweet Goody" to his pals, was there. I had been told he had died three years ago. It was great to see him. I invited him to church. He told me that he had to get some things in order. I informed him that we did not have that kind of church. The things that he wanted to get in order, he could bring them to church too. We joked for a moment, and then I left.

Duey walked me to the car without speaking. He appeared to still be in shock. Someone standing on the outside looking in would think that the shock was related to my beating him in billiards, but I knew in my heart that the shock was due to the fact that I had walked into the pool hall with him. And in the presence of all of those who knew his occupation, I still called him friend. He gave me a hug and I drove off.

2

THE HILL

I stopped at a buddy's house. His name was Grady Seigel. Grady was an old friend I had known for about twenty years. I met him when I moved to Charlotte back in 1979. He had been raised in the Baptist church, and from the time I met him I could tell that he had been whipped with religion. He was very knowledgeable and always susceptible to change. An incredible jazz musician, he had more vigor than ability—but he always seemed to make up for it with his knowledge of music theory. Grady really understood the principles of music. As I look back now, I can see that God placed Grady in my life to fine-tune some of the things that had been taught to me in years past.

In Grady's latter years, he joined the Catholic church. He always said that the church community never accepted him for being who he really was. But at Our Lady of Consolation they really didn't care. Grady was getting old and had suffered a stroke. But he always found the strength to encourage me and love me, regardless of his own condition. I dropped in to check on him and jokingly remind him of our midnight rides back in the day. Twenty years ago, at the same hour, I would have been in one of the local bars playing tunk or gin, as if I were king of the card table. Grady was my partner. He showed me all the sneaky tricks of the trade. After winning the house, we would ride out in the car and dream like children waiting for Christmas. Grady assured me that because of my ability to believe, I would one day reach my goals.

Stepping off of his porch, he told me to be careful. He respected my desire to touch other lives but was concerned about the hour and time that I chose to minister. I told him that I loved him and headed back to Double Oaks.

It was about 1:45 A.M. The strip clubs were jumping, and the liquor houses were overwhelmed with the sound of slow-walking blues. The prostitutes roamed the streets as if they were models on a New York runway. This particular night was my time to head up on the Hill, where the drug trafficking was at an all-time high. There were practically no lights on the Hill. This helped make it an ideal place to do late-night business. I noticed five guys standing by a tree. When I pulled up, the youngest one ran to my car and asked me what I needed. I told him I just wanted to hang out on the Hill for a minute.

I knew two of the guys—Raheem Blackmon and Tim Raymond, better known as "Red Dog." The other two men appeared a little annoyed that I was there. Each of the guys looked as though he had been sampling his contraband.

I assured them I would not be there long. "I don't want to scare your customers away," I said with a smile. "I just want to kick a little knowledge before I go home."

As I approached them, Red Dog introduced me to the three guys I did not know—without revealing their names. "This is my pastor," he said. Red Dog was a young man whom I had spent a lot of time mentoring. He had been around me since moving there from Peoria, Illinois. He was a young rapper and at one time had a clear vision of what he wanted out of life. But he had been side-tracked by the hype of the streets. Still, I loved him. Despite his backsliding, he had never disrespected me. I knew he was a young man whom God had marked, and it was only a matter of time before he would be snatched into the kingdom like I was twenty years ago.

I spoke with them for several minutes and held their attention. I asked them for twenty minutes of their time and promised that if they would hear me out, I would be on my way.

Red Dog looked embarrassed. "It's not like that," he said. "It's your 'hood just like it is ours. You can chill up here with us. We aren't doing anything wrong."

He knew I wasn't buying that. Earlier, I had seen two cars pull up to them and two transactions take place. What's more, it was obvious that they were as high as Mount Everest. With a smile on my face, I told him that I could have been the police. I warned them that there was indeed a cost for their actions. I let them know that *Scarface* wasn't just a movie and most of those who tried to mimic the lifestyles portrayed in that film are locked down doing twenty-five to life. In other words, the wages of sin is not freedom and life but imprisonment and death. Red Dog dropped his face in shame. I told him to lift up his head because I did not come to judge him or his cohorts. It was my job to let him know that God not only loves him but has a purpose for his life.

Red Dog's buddy, Raheem, was an old player in the street. I called him a merchant without a store. All you had to do was let him know where it was, what color you liked, and the size you needed and he would have it within forty-eight hours. Twenty years earlier, Raheem had stood beside me when one of my friends was gunned down approximately five blocks from the Hill. He knew the ugliness of the street, but he had sadly surrendered to its tyranny.

As I shared my testimony, Raheem suddenly interrupted. He told me that it was unfair for me to come and give these brothers false hope. There was no way that they could leave the corner and get out of the 'hood, he said. I looked Raheem squarely in the eyes and told him and the others that there are consequences for all that they do on the Hill. "The reality is that you place yourselves in the position to either be locked up, forced to rat on somebody, or dead. And then the cycle continues."

"Shut up and let him finish," Red Dog told Raheem. I didn't know if Red Dog wanted me to finish because he wanted to hear what I had to say or because he wanted me to hurry up and get out of there so that they could continue their work for the evening.

About that time the young boy who had run up to my car—whose name, I learned later, was Tony—became very agitated. It was as though my presence made him uncomfortable. So I said, "Listen, let me pray for you guys, then I'll leave."

Everybody agreed except for the two men I did not know. Well, they agreed . . . They were just reluctant to grab hands. But they finally did it anyway. We formed a circle, joined hands, and I began to ask God to come into their lives. Three or four minutes into the prayer, I looked at Tony and discovered that he was looking over my shoulder. Then the unthinkable happened.

3

ARRESTED

Little Tony broke from the circle and began to run as though a Rottweiler were chasing him. As I looked over my shoulder to see what he was running from, I found myself being taken to the ground in a WWF-style wrestling move. Three policemen had come out of nowhere, and they were placing all of us under arrest. Two of the guys were forced against my car and searched. Red Dog and Raheem were so high they didn't even know what was going on. The cops had rolled up from behind the building. I was startled, of course. But I cannot say that I was afraid. I knew my purpose there.

They immediately separated us and began their interrogation. After explaining who I was and why I was there, I was disappointed at the rudeness of the cop who questioned me. His name was Detective Anthony Sloan. He was known as a mild-mannered cop, but he hated the drug dealing in the inner city. His assistant was Detective T. D. Miller, a hard-nosed cop from Newark, New Jersey, who had an attitude with me from the beginning. When I finally got up from the ground, handcuffed, I noticed that the cop who had chased Tony came back empty-handed. Next, the policeman began reading us our rights. At this point, I was starting to become impatient—I had more ministry to tend to that evening.

Then, just when I thought things couldn't get worse, they did. The cops discovered individually wrapped packs of crack cocaine on the two men I did not know. So they were not only charged with possession of an illegal drug, but also with the intent to sell.

Red Dog and Raheem were so high and panicked that they could not answer any questions, and they became very uncooperative with the officers. The policeman who had failed to capture Tony was visibly agitated and began to make a lot of negative comments.

I asked the detective why I was being detained. He said, "I don't know what you guys were passing to each other, but we saw something pass from your hand to theirs."

I looked up. "Are you serious?"

"We photographed the transaction."

"I pray it's on video so that we can examine it and show you your inaccuracy," I said. I assured him that when our hands met, we were preparing to pray in a circle.

Sergeant Miller laughed arrogantly. "Do you expect me to believe that?" Before placing me in his car, Miller looked at me and said, "It's over."

Before I knew it we were all headed for the Mecklenburg County Jail. Once there, they carried me into a dark room, and we sat around a round table. The room was freezing. I complained, and they assured me I would not be there long. "Not long" turned into eight hours. They asked me the same question over and over: What was my affiliation with Red Dog, Raheem, and the other two guys?

The other two men, I later discovered, were Corey C and Michael H. I thought I had convinced the policemen that I had never met Corey or Michael, but Detective Miller was not buying it. Every time I told him that I was there as a minister of the Gospel, he made negative comments like, "Yeah, right! Try it again. I've heard that before."

Though I was uncomfortable at first, as the evening went on, I began to feel at peace with the situation. Truth is, as I look back at it now, I really got a kick out of the whole experience. It gave me the opportunity to testify to two detectives who could not comprehend the thought of a person wanting to help others, after midnight, in a place like Double Oaks.

Around eight o'clock that morning, Detective Miller stood up, slammed his hand on the table, and said, "All right Kee, while questioning Michael H and Corey C, we found out that you are not only the supplier; you have been running this drug operation for some time now."

I started to laugh in disbelief—and because I understood his strategy. Even if he felt I was not guilty, the fact that I was there, on the Hill, meant I knew something. So by accusing me, he felt I would talk. The ensuing questions made it clear to me that they had been following and watching me for some time.

They showed me pictures of properties that I own, and Miller even made the comment, "How could you gain so much in such a little time?" I was asked many questions about the business of drug trafficking, and I did not deny knowing how drugs were sold and the names of some of the people brought up in the investigation. This made Detective Sloan very enthusiastic, and I thought I saw him look at Detective Miller and say, "We got him this time."

This was not my first time being brought in for questioning. About ten years ago I had been followed for two days, brought in, and asked some of the same questions. Because of my testimony and willingness to share with others who I used to be and what I used to do, the officers were frankly puzzled—and angry. But I was still not prepared for what happened next.

I was booked and placed under arrest in violation of North Carolina General Statute 90-95-A1—"a felony possession to manufacture, sell, or possess, with intent to sell a controlled substance."

I called my wife, Felice, and assured her that everything was

OK. I told her to contact our attorneys. I also told her to contact my manager, Jeanette Taylor, and prepare her for a media frenzy. Felice was a little upset at first. But because of my innocence and the fact that she understood and knew my call, she was able to maintain a measure of peace that would be appreciated in times to come. I told her to take care of our six kids—Tredell, eight months, John-John, three, Aieisha, fifteen, Shannon, sixteen, Christopher, seventeen, and Justin, seventeen—and let them know that Daddy was OK and would see them in a few days.

The following Monday there was a bond hearing. My bond was set at $250,000. My attorneys and I were outraged. But then a still small voice spoke to me and said, "This is God's plan." On principle, I decided not to post bond and chose to stay in jail. In order to do this, I realized that I would need a few people on the outside to cover for me. As David and Jonathan had a blood covenant relationshipin the Old Testament, I too had one with my friend and Christian brother Regi Miner. I told him that if anything were ever to happen to me, one of the things I would want him to do is take care of my family.

Regi and I had known each other for fourteen years. Through smart investments and concrete foundational business practices, the Lord blessed us and gave us a sense of stability to reinvest in our vision to serve Him in the inner city. I was allowed to call Regi and update him on everything that had occurred thus far. I asked him for his true opinion. He told me he understood my stand, but he was concerned first about my family, and secondly about my church. I assured him that his opinion was important to me and that was the reason I had called him. I knew if he gave me his word, he would do everything to keep it. We had a silent partner named Carla Reed, who had worked with us in the area of video production. She was a sharp, intelligent lady and a program director for a national black entertainment firm. Since we were in the middle of production on several projects, Regi suggested that I call Carla and get her opinion.

Carla had a different take on matters. She felt that my arrest was dumb and didn't make sense. I should pay the bail, get out of jail, and deal with it at a later date, she advised. I stayed on the phone with her for an hour. I absolutely could not alter her opinion. Still, she promised that she would take care of what she could and place everything else on hold until this situation was cleared.

I shared with Regi and Carla that I would ask Elder Ben Truesdale, a close friend and business partner, and my older brother, Alphonza Kee, to cover the church. There were a few other associate ministers who would assist them in any way necessary.

Ben was one of the chief negotiators for the church and my ministry's corporate business affairs. I knew he was somebody I could trust to keep things in order.

Then there was my brother Alphonza. He was not your everyday preacher, but he had successfully run a program in our church called One Step. The One Step program was designed to compensate for some of the shortcomings of our nation's twelve-step programs. I found that people who had come out of twelve-step programs had received an abundance of facts and information but lacked a true sense of God's power or authority to bring healing to their lives. I knew that the only power strong enough to help a person overcome an addiction to cocaine was Jesus Christ. I didn't know this by reading materials, pamphlets, or watching *New Jack City*. I knew it by experience and through my own testimony. From cocaine to prescription tranquilizers, I had been locked in bondage and needed a way out. I have been clean for twenty years now, and I know in my heart that the only true deliverance comes in having a personal relationship with the Lord Jesus Christ.

Under Al's leadership, our One Step program became a huge success. We've helped hundreds of individuals find victory over their addictions. I knew that if I had to stay incarcerated for two or three months, Al had the wisdom and vision to keep the church's ministry on track. This in no way was intended to shun the other ministers. But I knew that Al would not bring another dream into a vision that was already working.

Regi promised that he would be by my side and would catch the next flight from D.C. to Charlotte. Al's response, however, was a bit different. I called him and explained the situation and how I would like to handle it. His response stunned me a little, because I did not know he would take it to heart. Let me explain.

Growing up, Al was the brother who never showed emotion. But that was not the case that day. In his voice I could detect anger, sadness, and perhaps a bit of trepidation. I had to determine in a hurry whether Al's apparent resistance to my plan was a reaction to my being locked up or simply fear of what he would have to endure while taking over the church. Soon enough, though, I knew it was the fact that his baby brother would be locked down for a couple of months. He told me not to worry about the church. He felt like he could handle it.

By this time, the news of my arrest had been on every local station and in every local paper. I asked Al about the response of the people in the church. He told me that most folks were standing behind me. But, of course, there were a few who were talking to the media and making statements like "I never trusted him" and "It figures; nobody comes back to the neighborhood and spends as much time as he did hanging out on the streets."

Al said, "Don't worry about it. Stay focused and remember what you always tell the congregation: *On the other side of this is indeed a blessing.*"

He told me he had visited Felice and the kids. They were fine. I told him to contact my mother and grandmother and inform them about the nature of the charges and what had really happened. He told me he had already done that and whatever my decision, he would stand by me.

When my attorneys arrived, there were additional issues to be ironed out. "This bond is ridiculous," I told them.

I knew that I was innocent of all charges. I had to stand my ground. Two of my attorneys, Max Siegel and Keith Cunningham, agreed with me, but William Kee, a first cousin who was in charge of my financial affairs, felt that we should pay the bond and call it a day. I felt by not paying the bond I would make a major statement to the authorities—and I felt a tugging on my heart to just trust God. Although William disagreed with me, he promised to support my decision and do whatever was necessary to get a speedy trial.

On Monday morning I was indicted by the grand jury. My case was going to trial. My attorneys assured me that because of the nature of the charges and the rush to judgment from the district attorney's office to clean up the inner city, we would get a prompt trial.

I finally called my wife to tell her about my outrageous bond. I had no idea how she would respond. When I told her, she began to cry. She stated that it did not make sense. I asked her how she would feel about my staying in jail until the trial. I told her that by seeing this thing through, we would make a major statement and that God would get the glory out of this ordeal.

"I support your decision," she told me gently. "I love you. The kids and I will be fine."

With Felice's approval, I set my sights toward the goal of enduring incarceration for some greater good. God, I believed, would show me my purpose there in due time.

"Locked up in P.O.D. 3200"

"Pastor teaches behind prison walls"

"Harris captivates the Defense"

"Detective Anthony Sloan on the stand"

"D.A. Harris plans strategy"

"Max and William revisit crime scene"

"NOT GUILTY"

*"After brief news conference
Pastor Kee leaves courthouse"*

4

LOCKED DOWN

I was taken to Spencer Drive, a jail facility approximately three miles from our church. They treated me well there. At least three of the jailers attended my church. One of them did not speak to me. Apparently, he believed the accusations leveled against me. The other two jailers, however, made my stay as comfortable as possible. I asked them to do me a favor upon my arrival; I asked them not to give me any special privileges. I told them that I believed God had me there for a reason and although it was not my choice, it was my course. I learned the next day that my stay there could be as long as two months. If that turned out to be the case, I decided that it would be two months that I could use to study God's Word and to listen intently for His voice.

I was placed in a temporary holding area where the inmates were either waiting to be arraigned or to be assigned to their P.O.D. (Place of Detention). The holding area was supposed to house about forty-eight men, but there were presently sixty-two. When I arrived there, it was time for one of the daily roll calls. A jailer and his assistant stood at designated spots, and the inmates lined up in a quarter-circle when our names were called and showed the officers our wristbands. Ironically, there were a lot of church people locked up at that facility. I saw people I hadn't seen for years, and I'm sure none of us ever imagined that we'd see one another again—let alone under these circumstances.

I asked one of the jailers if he had any clue as to why I was in the holding area. "I'm not supposed to tell you this," he said, "but because of the charges against you, they're trying to determine whether you should be placed in G.P. (the general population) or in protective custody."

I knew that the holding area was equipped with enough bunks to sleep forty-eight men. Since there were sixty-two of us that night, I was anxious to see where everyone was going to sleep. Many of the inmates knew me, either from my days on the street or from my outreach ministry in Double Oaks, so they made sure I got a bunk. It wasn't very comfortable, but it was better than the cold cement floor. The next morning, we were awakened at six o'clock. I was informed that I had been assigned to a Place of Detention. They took me, shackled like a criminal, to P.O.D. 3200. There they gave me my own cell. I made it just in time for the early-morning shift change and roll call.

After the roll call, the inmates sat down in the Day Room and prepared for an orientation, where the jail officials explained the rules and regulations of the facility: No music, no videos, keep the noise level down, keep your gym suit tucked in, no visiting rooms, etc. The officer who read the orientation information was a regular attendee of my church. His name was Officer Antonio Love. When I walked around to show him my wristband I was tickled to hear him say, in a whisper, "Good morning, Pastor."

I did not say anything; I just smiled and took my seat. The guy in the cell next to mine was a young man by the name of Handel Menendez, known as "Big Handy" because of his imposing physical stature. He stood about 6'8", and he cast a shadow every time he walked by. He was a young brother like many of the brothers there who were incarcerated and claimed that they were there on false pretenses. In other words, he said he was not guilty.

He said angry friends who were upset that he was out of the drug trade had railroaded him.

Handy and I had several conversations. It was mostly me sharing the Gospel and my experiences with him. But I must say, as I look back at it now, God used him to pass a lot of knowledge to me as well. I told him how much the streets had changed and how, in my day, even in our sin and wrongdoing, there was a code of ethics—an element of integrity—that is nonexistent today. The little jail time that I had done in my past was actually done for something that I did not do, but back then I would rather serve time for something I did not do than have the cops inquire about what I was *really* doing. If I had squealed on a few of my friends, I could have walked free. But we had a motto back then: "Don't get mad at the player; get mad at the game." In those days, I was more upset about getting busted than about the depraved lifestyle I was leading.

Handy listened to me intently. He had an open spirit and seemed hungry for godly counsel. Though I felt that his tactics on the streets were senseless, I was able to take my past and minister to his present.

Officer Love walked over and told me that I would have to sign up for one of four jobs—cleaning the bathroom, sweeping and mopping the Day Room, cleaning the glass windows and walls, or food cart and trash takeout. Love smiled and told me that he would try to get me on food cart and trash takeout because the officer who would bring the food up was a tenor in our church choir named Darius O. Frederick. He told me that Darius had been worrying him all day. "How is Pastor Kee? What is he doing? Is he OK?"

"I assured Darius that you were OK and that I was keeping a close eye on you," Officer Love said. As he began to walk away, I tapped him on the shoulder and said to him again, "No special treatment." He seemed to ignore me and walked off.

Years before, at night in our bedroom, when the lights were off, my brother Alphonza taught me something about music notation. Though I was locked down, I was able to write many songs and remember songs and lyrics by a number system that Al had devised. I had not released an album in approximately three years. I knew that I would have to record one soon. I started to laugh and said to myself, *This whole experience could be put into melodic form, with a title cut called "Not Guilty."* As I thought about it, my smile turned serious. Yes, perhaps this experience was to be the inspiration for a new project that God had already predestined for me.

* * *

My jail time offered me countless opportunities to minister. Whether at dinner or out in the jail yard, it was almost as if I were a doctor at a hospital full of needy patients. As my fellow inmates got to know me, they actually believed that I had the cure for what ailed them. Everywhere I went, when I spoke they listened. It started to look like a daily walking revival. This annoyed some of the jailers, who pulled me aside and asked if I could limit my group gatherings. I was praying for inmates, praying for families, praying for children, praying for fathers, praying for spiritual deliverance, and God was moving in a mighty way. And each night He would give me another song based on my daily encounters. When friends, members of my church, or my attorneys would come to visit me and ask me how I was doing, some of them could not understand my upbeat demeanor.

One afternoon, I was sitting at one of the corner tables in the Day Room reading a letter from my daughter Shannon when two officers approached me. The look on their faces suggested that I was in some type of trouble.

One of the officers looked down at me and said, "Mr. Kee, we have an issue that concerns us greatly. It appears that you are receiving a considerable amount of mail. To be honest with you, you are receiving more mail than the entire P.O.D. Is there any way that you could contact your church, family, or office and have your fan mail, as well as some of your church mail, sent to another location?"

He was very courteous. I was not offended and even thought that it was a very nice gesture for him to come to me and ask me. I had been incarcerated for approximately one month and the mail had been coming in enormous amounts. From California to Maine, from Hawaii to Nigeria, it appeared that my story had touched a nerve. There were well-wishers, sympathizers, and those who simply wanted to offer a heartening word. Every other day there would be one or two letters from those who were convinced I was guilty. But the majority of the letters were very encouraging.

To tell the truth, it was hard to keep up with all that mail. Between reading and trying to respond, it was becoming a full-time job. I thanked the officer for bringing this to my attention. Then the assistant officer standing just behind him made a negative comment. He looked at me and said, "I didn't know that being a drug dealer and a preacher came with such popularity."

I wasn't in the mood to dignify this statement with a reply. But I took a deep breath, stood up, squared my shoulders, stared him right in his face, and said, "My brother, don't allow your personal jailhouse gossip to be confused with God's favor."

I thanked both of them and turned and walked away. This particular officer seemed to have a problem with me from day one. But after that simple exchange of words, he began to speak to me with more respect, and this developed into a somewhat friendly relationship. For me, it was just another example of God's Spirit moving to bring good from bad.

One of the letters I received that day was from Elder Ben Truesdale. He told me that a piece of property we had been looking at for the school had become available. This particular property was located on the west side of Double Oaks. It was a five-acre lot and we had regularly been in touch with the owner to purchase it. Ben not only gave me great news that day by telling me it was available, but he told me that that he had bid on the land and the owner agreed to sell. So there was nothing that day that would allow me to hold my head down. For even in the midst of my imprisonment, God was doing exciting things.

I spoke to the chaplain of the jail and he allowed me to minister one Sunday morning. It was one of the most memorable experiences of my time there. Young brothers from cults and non-Christian beliefs actually surrendered their lives to the Lord Jesus that day. Indeed, what a mighty God we serve.

There was a white inmate there by the name of Lorenzo Brown. He had been locked up for attempted murder and like many of us there was preparing to go to trial. He was tattooed from his shoulders to his fingers. He oftentimes boasted about his white separatist views, yet he had become very bitter because he felt betrayed by some of the brothers in the movement. Though I tried to reach out to him, he always seemed to have a problem with me. He started a rumor that I was on the inside as an undercover informant trying to gain information to take to the powers that be. When one of the guards brought this to my attention, I approached Lorenzo and began to share my heart. It was not long before I recognized the obvious: The only thing that stood between Lorenzo and me was fear—fear and ignorance.

I was taught—and I teach—that ignorance is simply not being informed. The more we shared about our differences, the more I found out that we were just alike. He had been raised in the church and many of the things that he had already been delivered from he felt he should put on a shelf never to be seen or heard from again. I told him the things that he wanted to hide could be the very things that God wants to use to bring him healing and deliverance. It was through witnessing to this brother that I found out that many of the things God delivers us from keep us enslaved for years to come. We don't fully accept the fact that the blood of Jesus washes us and cleanses us from *all* unrighteousness. We don't have to hold on to guilt from the past.

I also told him that many in the church were responsible for perverting the word *sanctified*. The prophets of old knew without a doubt in their minds that *sanctified* in Hebrew, Latin, and Greek literally meant "to cleanse." Church folks perverted it when they taught that cleansing means "separating from." Through the years, they "separated from" by saying we are more religious than those people, or that if someone doesn't shout, dance, pray, and sing as we do, then they are not in God's will. I explained to Lorenzo that God would not only cleanse him of all of his unrighteousness; He would also give him the grace and vision to go back into the world and live a godly life. I used myself as an example. There was no reason for me to be in jail, I told him. But as I looked at God's call on my life, I understood that it was the place I needed to be.

5

I SHALL NOT
BE INTIMIDATED

Officer Love approached me one day and told me to be careful. It had been rumored that I would soon be placed in protective custody because there was an inmate in P.O.D. 2200 who was going to testify against me at the trial. This not only startled me but, for a brief moment, it seemed impossible. There was no one, other than the five who stood on the Hill with me that night, who had witnessed what took place. And to my knowledge, I had not wronged or offended any of them. It was ironic that Officer Love would say something to me that day, because earlier in the day an inmate whom I had known from years past approached me in the Day Room. I could not say that we were friends, but we were acquaintances. He was working along with me cleaning the bathrooms. His street name was "Gizzard." He was a young man who used to live in Clanton Park, a Charlotte housing development. He told me that a young man approached him in the infirmary and asked him if I had been doing any talking. "I told him that you have been encouraging us and as for what you were in here for, nobody really knew," Gizzard said.

I could tell that he was feeling me out. I didn't know if it was for the inmate in P.O.D. 2200 or for the prosecutors. So, I gave him something real good to take back to them. I told him I believed all of this took place so that I might have this conversation with him in the bathroom. I told him that on that particular night, I would start singing and praying about midnight and the jail walls would begin to shake and crumble. Then, I was going to walk to my crib. He looked at me like I was crazy and never said anything else to me.

* * *

I had been locked up for three months. It was June. I was about a week away from my trial, and I was beginning to really feel my humanness. It was as though everything that had happened and was happening had come to intimidate me. I cannot define the emotions, but I rested in one thing: I still believed that I was called to be who I was. And after years of teaching the congregation about purpose by design, I knew that God was still in control.

Here are some random selections from my journal that week:

Today I wrote a song called "Rhema Word." After writing the lyrics, I smiled to myself and sensed God's Spirit in the song. The first line in the song says, "Send a word in the tabernacle." One would ask, "How could you call a jail cell a tabernacle?" My answer would simply be, "Wherever I am, He is." This cell has become the tabernacle of prayer. Big Handy, who at one time would never even bless his food, is now praying and believing God to step in the midst of his trial and render him Not Guilty. The second verse of the song says to send a word into the tabernacle that we might recognize that we have been acquitted and by faith we are justified. Can you believe it? Lorenzo Brown, who was a teenage skinhead, is totally convinced that the sins of his past are just that, the sins of his past. He has been acquitted and he is witnessing with a vengeance. I could tell that he had a lot of knowledge of the Word of God, but I am glad I can testify that this Word that is in his spirit is now applicable. We have been acquitted from the stain of guilt and shame. It is the guilt and the shame that keeps many in bondage. I believe that when we truly embrace the cleansing power of the blood of Jesus, the shame will leave. When the shame leaves, we will hold our heads up and pronounce to a dying nation that we are NOT GUILTY.

* * *

One of the guards was busted today for trafficking. And the men on the yard were acting like this was a wonderful thing. I was able to use that as a tool to minister to a lot of the brothers and remind them that the devil hates them—that regardless of our position, if we are not prayed up, we can fall into Satan's snare. Instead of laughing and joking, I told them, we needed to love this brother. So we all grabbed hands and began to lift him up in prayer.

* * *

Three days before trial, believe it or not, I know in my heart I will be acquitted. I have written almost thirty songs. I can't wait to get in the studio and see where God takes me with this. Normally, I just write ideas, but this time it is like the No. 7 just smacked me upside my head—I continue to hear the words completion and accuracy.

* * *

I ran into a guy today by the name of Frank S, whose street name is "Speedball." Speedball was doing forty to life for trafficking enough heroin to supply the Eastern seaboard. He had been sent down from the state to testify in a new trial. I met him approximately twenty years ago. He was a first cousin of Raheem. He seemed overjoyed to see me. This was strange because it was unorthodox for someone like him to be overly happy to see another brother. It was not until he opened his mouth that I understood why he was overjoyed. When I called him Speedball, he immediately rebuked the thought and told me to call him Franklin. He had given his life over to the Lord and did not want to be called by old aliases that were associated with his illegal conduct.

He had been serving approximately eighteen years in a prison in Raleigh. He told me he knew of all the good things that I had been doing in Charlotte and he was amazed to see me in an orange jumpsuit. I told him about the night in question and that instead of paying out an outrageous amount of money for bail, I decided to stay in jail. I told him that I truly believed that God had me here for a reason. I told him that I had a few more days before my court date, and that I was sure that I would be exonerated. He asked me many questions about the ministry. It was great to see him and even greater to know that he was on the Lord's side. Many talk a good game and pretend that they are saved, just to make their way easier on the inside. But Franklin was definitely on point. Twenty years ago, you could probably find Franklin's photo in the dictionary next to the word ruthless. *To see how God not only changed his nature, but his heart, was a true testimony. His compassion went before him and touched everyone he came in contact with.*

* * *

My attorney, Max Siegel, came to see me that evening. He told me that the D.A. wanted to meet with me to see if I would accept a plea bargain. This was hilarious to me, for I knew in my heart that I had done nothing wrong. Although the charges seemed strong, all of the evidence was circumstantial. As far as they were concerned, it just did not look right for a pastor to be out at that time of night and associating with those types of people.

I had a team of attorneys who knew me personally and fully understood my passion for ministry. Still, it was their job to let me know what my options were. Max shared some other things with me that were disturbing. As the state was preparing their case against me, it was as if they were pulling snakes out of the grass. One of the persons who would testify against me was an old real-estate acquaintance whom I had a major confrontation with in the past. You see, he had purchased some houses in the inner city and promised the tenants who had been renting for years that after the renovations, he would sell the properties to them, knowing that these people would not be able to qualify for the loans. But once the renovations were completed, they were evicted and literally run out of the neighborhood. He changed the name of the area and now it is a gated community. It appeared that nobody would stand up to him. When I moved back to this area, I made God a promise that my passion would be for the people. So at a neighborhood district meeting, when he stood up and proposed to buy homes of the elderly in a neighborhood very close to Double Oaks, I called him on the carpet.

I have always had a concern that as we tear down our housing to make our city more attractive for economic development, we are forgetting our citizens who have labored there for years. As we tear down the dilapidated housing projects and replace them with high-priced condos, where will our people move? As I look at the whole picture, it is frightening because as the projects are confiscated, the jails are getting larger.

As a pastor in the inner city, I have adopted a personal motto: "It is better to teach them now than to rehabilitate them later." Instead of building jails, I believe in my heart that I am called to build schools—so that our young men and women might be challenged and encouraged to know that their knowledge can propel them past their present circumstances.

What was this real-estate developer going to say? Max said he would testify that I secretly owned approximately forty-two acres in the inner city. That was odd because why would a pastor need property? We got a big laugh out of that.

Another person who would testify was Wanda W, a young

lady I met eleven years ago when she came to an inner-city soft-ball game with her child. To make a long story short, her son and I hit it off. The young man's name was Quincy. I had taken him under my wing, but it appeared that later in life Quincy had a certain attraction to the streets. I tried to get him help many times by getting him into rehab. But there was one problem: Although Quincy was willing to admit that he did have a crack cocaine problem, his mother was not.

Wanda had been raised in church and attended a local assembly in the Charlotte area. She was in charge of the witnessing program at her church and had praised the work that we were doing in Double Oaks. Quincy's father had been locked up for most of his son's life. I wanted to help him as much as I could. For ten years, I helped them with rent, bought school clothes, made car payments, bought them food, and brought a sense of stability to this young man and his surroundings.

Now that he was older, he began to steal to support his habit. His mother, for all of her biblical knowledge, refused to see it or to address it. It was time for tough love. Quincy had been in and out of jail since age fourteen. Now he was nearly twenty. Many people told me to give up on him a long time ago. But anytime I look at a child like Quincy, I think of my own testimony. It only takes one jarring episode to get some people's attention, and Quincy was that kind of child. I believed in my heart that he loved the Lord. He knew the Scripture from cover to cover. But he had a lot of knowledge without any commitment. As long as he was around the church or around my family, I never had to worry about him. But as soon as he would hit the streets, he felt like he owed the devil something. It was time to be stern. I made up my mind that until I had help from Quincy's mother, I could no longer baby-sit him.

One night Wanda called me begging for money. The way she begged was not normal. So I agreed to meet her at my office. She had always kept a job, and if there was a problem, you could count on her to be honest about it. She walked in with a girl by the name of Sheeka. I asked her if she wanted Sheeka to come in to the meeting too. She said no, she just didn't want to be out at night by herself. She then told me she needed a considerable amount of cash. Being from the old school, if someone needed money to pay a bill, I would rather pay the bill for her than give her cash. I continued to ask her what the money was for. She finally broke down and told me she had lost her job. She worked at a local cookie manufacturer. She had been there for fourteen years. I asked her how she lost her job. She told me her division had downsized. This sounded a little strange, but I continued to listen. She also told me that in order to make ends meet she had allowed this girl in the lobby, Sheeka, her two brothers, and the guy she was dating to move into her home.

I said, "Stop right there."

She interrupted, "No, I want to be honest." She told me she needed a large amount of money because she owed Sheeka $600. I asked her how she could owe Sheeka $600 if Sheeka was the one living with her. She said it was for a gambling debt. That disturbed me because gambling was a problem that I had overcome in my own life—and, trust me, Wanda was no gambler. It was likely that her current boyfriend, a local hustler, brought this element around her, but I knew it was not Wanda's nature. The stories did not add up. I asked Wanda where Quincy was. She told me he was at home with her boyfriend. This concerned me, and I did not attempt to conceal this from Wanda.

This made her furious. She called me judgmental—and a few other names that I'd rather not remember. She said if she did not get the money from me she would lose her house. Then she threatened to never let me see Quincy again and told me to stay away from him. This was not the Wanda I knew. She stormed out of my office and slammed the door. She and Sheeka left the building.

On the way home that night, I stopped at a gas station, where I ran into a known dealer whom I had been witnessing to for about three years. Before I could speak to him, he made a comment: He told me to tell Wanda to stop coming by his house.

I thought Wanda had been witnessing, so I made the comment to him, "Why don't you give in and go to church with her and she will leave you alone?"

"That's not what I'm talking about," he said. "Wanda never tells me to come to church. I want you to talk to her because I cannot stand to see a mother get high with her son."

I was shocked. That was the day I discovered that the demon of crack cocaine does not discriminate.

I left the gas station and immediately went to Wanda's house and confronted her. She started to cry. I told her if she wanted help, I could get it for her, but if she stayed in denial, I would have to sever all ties. This would prove to be one of the toughest decisions I ever made—not because of the shock of finding out that Wanda was smoking, too, but because I knew I was one of the few people she and Quincy would ever confide in.

Wanda began to curse and blame me for every problem that she'd ever had. Being a pastor, this was familiar territory for me. Many times, before finding a road to deliverance, we blame everybody for our failures. Wanda finally said something that angered me; she said if I had been there for her son, he wouldn't have started smoking crack. This concerned me because this was one child I had really spent quality time with and many times deprived my own children of time just so he would not become another statistic. She knew her comment was not true.

She possibly forgot the troubled neighborhood she herself lived in and said, "If I had never taken him to Double Oaks, he would have never been introduced to the element of life that tangled him."

"Are you accusing me of Quincy's drug involvement?" I asked.

"Yeah."

I assured her that I would be praying for her. She told me not to waste my breath. I had always thought of Wanda as a sister. I gave her credit for standing in the midst of storms. So I was particularly hurt when I learned she would be testifying against me.

When my attorney told me, it was the first time in the whole ordeal that I began to feel bitterness.

I said to Max, "Please give me some good news."

He assured me that he had stopped and checked on my wife before coming over and the family was doing great. He told me that my little boy John-John really wanted to see me. But I had made my wife make a promise that she would not bring the children to the jail to see me. I had not called in the last three days, because the last phone call was very painful. My son had seen me on TV the Sunday prior, and my wife told me that he cried for more than an hour. I cannot tell you what was going on with me emotionally at that time. This was the day I remember. It appeared that everything was falling apart. But again, I remembered where my joy comes from.

Max also assured me that Al and Ben were taking good care of the church. That was great news. Max told me that there were a few other things he needed to tell me before he left. He informed me that there had been another development in the prosecution's case against me. This amazed me because I knew that I had done nothing that evening. In fact, I had often wondered what real evidence the cops had to charge me with. I found out that day that one of the young men whom I did not know had testified to the grand jury that he was there to sell me cocaine. Max told me that this story was corroborated by Tony, the young man who ran away.

I asked Max, "Did they catch him?"

"Evidently."

Now the puzzle was finally coming together. I suddenly remembered when Gizzard had spoken to me, as we cleaned the bathrooms, about a young man questioning my dialogue with the brothers. Until that day I had never believed in the notion of a conspiracy, but something was not right.

Still, there remained a peace in me that I knew was a gift from God. I was reminded of Isaiah 26:3—"You will keep him in perfect peace, whose mind is stayed on You" (NKJV). I was filled with that very peace. And, like never before, I stood on the Word of God, knowing that God would not give me more than I could handle (1 Corinthians 10:13).

As Max and I spoke, my cousin and attorney William Kee entered the room to tell me about a proposed plea bargain. He told me they were willing to offer me a lighter sentence if I would turn state's evidence on Raheem and admit that I was on the Hill that night purchasing cocaine. I waited to hear William say that we should reject the offer, for if anybody knew that I was innocent, he did. He said nothing.

This concerned me. "So how do you want me to respond to this?" I asked him.

He snapped and said, "Listen, John, this is hard on all of us. If we cooperate and work together, we can get through it together. This is not my offer; this is the state's offer. If you want to discuss it further, we can meet with them. But as your attorney, it is my job to bring it to the table. Your guilt or innocence has nothing to do with this conversation. Although I still feel that you should pay the bail and get out of here."

I looked at Max and asked him, "So how much cocaine was actually found on these guys?" He said it had to be over thirty bags, because there were two charges of possession with intent to sell. I asked him if there was any word on what Raheem or Red Dog were saying.

"There are two positive things I wanted to tell you, and that was one of them," Max said. "Both Raheem and Red Dog have maintained that you were innocent and the only reason that you guys grabbed hands was to pray."

The second thing was that the trial had been moved to the neighboring town of Monroe for security reasons. My attorneys had requested this move. Max was elated about this turn of events. Frankly, I couldn't have cared less. But because my lawyers were happy, I was happy too. We grabbed hands and thanked God. Then they left.

On my way back to my cell, one of the guards asked for my

autograph. I had been reluctant to give it thus far because I knew that was not my purpose in jail. As he gave me the pen, I discovered that he did not want my autograph at all. He told me he just wanted to encourage my heart. He said his sister lived in the Double Oaks area and that she would always remember the time our church brought farm animals into the inner city and hosted a small petting zoo. We had allowed the children in Double Oaks to experience something they had never experienced. The guard's sister said they not only had a good time, but that the hands-on experience had changed her young son's life. He assured me that he had been looking over my shoulder to make sure that I was OK. If I needed anything, he said, I should let him know. He told me that he would be praying for me. Then he locked me up.

6

ENCOURAGED

When I got to my cell I noticed that the piece of paper he gave me was rather large for an autograph and he did not ask for it back. I opened it up and it was a letter from his nephew. The writing was somewhat broken and distorted, but I could understand it:

> Pastor Kee,
> I really love you. You have been there for me time and time again. And I want you to know that I am there for you. I am praying for you and I know that everything is going to be OK. You taught us at church about acts of faith. You told us when we needed something we could write it down and every day speak as though it is already here. That is why I know you will be set free.
> Your friend, Desmond Taylor.

As corny as this letter may sound, this was the encouragement I needed. God is so amazing. I am constantly in awe of His sovereignty and impeccable timing. He is always on time. Before closing my eyes that night, I kept humming the words, "My God will do what He wants to whenever He wants to; He is God." I could not go to sleep. I envisioned the choir walking on stage. It was a large choir, one of a size that I had never seen before, and they began to sing "Sovereign" over and over again. I committed the song to my memory. Then I was out for the night.

The next morning I woke up to the same routine—early-morning roll call and orientation. I couldn't believe it, but they were reading the same rules over again. I knew my days there were numbered. If there was anything that I had to do in that place, it had to be done within the next forty-eight hours. This particular morning, in my meditation, I began to thank God for preserving me through this ordeal.

In my cell I had a few pictures that kept me strengthened and encouraged. One was a picture of my family. In this particular picture, Tredell, my youngest son, was approximately two months old. The other kids sat around Felice and me. I call this photo "The Picture of Hope." Every time I looked at it, I thanked God for covering and keeping my family while I was locked up.

I had received many letters, and every time I received a letter I would be insulted because I wasn't the first person to read it. Yes, it is true: All of the mail that one receives in jail is opened and searched. I guess it is necessary, but it still leaves you feeling violated. My wife had written me approximately thirty-three times. I could tell in her letters that she honestly wanted me to pay the bail and get out, but she respected my decision and continued to pray for me.

Chaplain James Day came by to see me at about 4:30 that afternoon, and I was blessed by his visit. He shared with me that many of the inmates had been encouraged and blessed by my being there. He said that he did not know the particulars of the case and that he did not care. Then he shared a few stories from the apostle Paul's letters. We prayed and he left.

I called home to check on my family. My wife began to ask me questions about the trial, which was only a few days away. She asked me if I was prepared. I began to share with her some of the information that was relayed to me by my attorneys.

She politely interrupted and said, "I wasn't talking about the physical; I was talking about the spiritual."

She wanted to know if I was OK spiritually. I told her I was tiring a little and was ready for the trial. Before we hung up, we ran through a little ritual that we had developed since my incarceration. I would say, "What's the verdict?" And she would respond, "Not guilty." This time, I really needed to hear that.

7

GOD'S INTENTION

An entry from my journal:

It is my last day in G.P. (general population), and believe it or not, as much as I miss home, my family, and friends, I believe I will probably miss this place. There is something about deliverance that excites me. This area of ministry is what I have always believed I was called to do. This was much different from an altar call in a church or the dust around the podium at an outdoor revival. This was face-to-face, every day, with real issues that I have experienced or seen with my natural eye.

As I look back at this brief stay, I can't say that it was a holiday, but I believe in my heart that everything God intended to be took place. There are a few who still feel my testimony is out of order. But as I said to them, and as I still feel now, my approach is not intimidation but love. I just want to spread the love of God in this time of personal exile.

To some, these walls will be revolving doors for the rest of their lives. They will use crime as an ultimate high, at the expense of others. But I do believe that there are some who will clearly see the light through the bricks.

Today I plan to do something that may seem a little corny to some. During roll call, the P.O.D. officer stands in one spot and we circle the room and show our bracelets. Yesterday, he allowed one of the inmates to assist him. Before Officer Love punched out yesterday, I asked him if there was any way possible that I could assist him the following day. He said that he did not see a problem with that. He began to walk away. He took three steps, turned around, and asked me why. I told him that I believed it would be my last day.

One of the other officers heard me and responded, "Yeah, I heard that if you were found guilty they were going to ship you straight out of city and into state."

I looked him in the eye and responded declaratively, "The only visit to Raleigh I'll take will be my family vacation to the state fair. After this trial, I am going home."

* * *

I will never forget that day. At 4:00 P.M., it was time for roll call. Officer Love called my name first. I showed him my wristband, and he asked me to stand beside him. This was not only a sentimental fantasy of mine; it gave me the opportunity that I longed for—to pray for God's blessing on the lives of all the men who were detained in P.O.D. 3200.

As he called the names alphabetically and the brothers walked by, I stared directly into their faces. To many I would utter the words, "Thank You, Jesus," to others, "Lord, cover them." By the time the eighth inmate passed me, it was clear that everybody knew why I was standing there and what I was doing. Tears streamed down the faces of grown men. It was that day that I saw the Spirit of God begin to cleanse hearts, alter destinies, and bind deep inner wounds. This was the day that I knew *Not Guilty* would be a CD, a book, and ultimately an experience that would touch the lives of every man and woman who came in contact with this opus. It was here that I envisioned the blood of Jesus setting free men with all manner of spiritual diseases. After about fourteen men had passed, tears were rolling down my face. There was something about those tears that humbled the room. There I was—6'1", 295 pounds, known around the jail as "Big Preacher" —with tears in my eyes, thanking God for His ability to rescue lost souls.

This blood that I had taught about, sung about, and danced about for years was not just for church people. God's desire to reach all souls became utterly clear to me. At times, I had begun to question this truth, saying to myself, *You mean to tell me God loves him too?* But at that moment I was filled with God's compassion to save every man. I tried to contain myself, for I knew if my words of blessing got any louder, Officer Love would ask me to take a seat. However, when I looked over to my left, he too was sobbing uncontrollably.

Out of all the concerts and all the church services I have attended in my life, there was absolutely nothing that could compare to what was going on in P.O.D. 3200. Officer Cliff Wyatt, who at one time had said he didn't find my religious antics conducive to prison life, was standing by the entrance door with his arms around himself, crying like a young child. I knew then, beyond a shadow of a doubt, that the power of God was in that place.

After the last name was called, I wiped my eyes and stepped out on faith to share my heart with the men in that room. "I leave tomorrow and many of you brothers I will never see again. But today is the beginning of the rest of our lives. Some of you have made choices, and now you are dealing with the reactions of your actions, but I want you to know that you still have a chance. Some are facing five years, some are facing twenty to life, but God has assured us, if you surrender your life to Him, you will not just be another inmate; you shall immediately become a child of the Lord. I don't have time to explain every detail of what that means, but I will tell you this: If you will commit your life to Jesus Christ, no weapon formed against you shall prosper. The Bible says in Romans 10:9, "If thou shalt confess with thy mouth the Lord Jesus, and shalt believe in thine heart that God hath raised him from the dead, thou shalt be saved" (KJV). Once you surrender your life to God, you will become an heir to His kingdom. He will protect, cover, strengthen, and speak peace to your situation.

"I go to court tomorrow, some would say not knowing my fate. But by faith I believe God that I'll be at home in a few days. Brothers, do me a favor: When you receive the Lord, don't walk in His courtroom in fear, for fear is the opposite of faith. Instead, go in believing God that you are not only saved but He is in charge. And when you have been exonerated, don't forget the God who delivered you. I can't judge your sin, but I say to all of you right now, in Jesus Christ you are NOT GUILTY."

There had been a lot of preaching in P.O.D. 3200. We had several Bible studies while I was there, so it was not uncommon for all of us to be sitting down hearing the same Word simultaneously. But when it came to prayer, out of respect for other religions, the religious leaders would always say, "Just meditate quietly."

One of the Muslim brothers stationed in P.O.D. 3200 was a young man who grew up in the same neighborhood that I lived in when I moved to Charlotte. I knew him as "Junnie." He had since changed his name to Yucef Malik. Although we had different beliefs, he had great respect for me. We had become close years ago when he worked security for a secular R&B band that I briefly joined in the early '80s. I had no idea how he would respond to what I was about to do next.

I turned to Officer Love. "I know that we normally meditate," I said, "but if it's OK with all of the men here today, I would love to pray out loud that God would bless everybody standing."

Officer Love held up his head and immediately looked at Brother Yucef Malik. Yucef looked at me and nodded.

Officer Love said, "Does anybody object to this?" All of the brothers said no.

This was the opportunity of a lifetime. Those who are pastors and teachers know and understand the importance of the altar call. It is there where we not only surrender the things that are not like God but allow Him to come into our lives.

As I began to pray, I gave thanks for every man there. I asked God to deliver every man in that circle. I prayed for their families and their situations. For a moment it felt like P.O.D. 3200 had been transformed into the Upper Room. God's presence had enveloped us in such a way that we were all in one accord.

I've worked in the music business for many years, yet I have always disliked being around photographers and video cameras. But I wish this one day could have been recorded. Not only did the men praise God, but they all followed my lead and repeated a simple sinner's prayer. Immediately following the prayer, the brothers began to embrace. I was sure that the officers would step in and bring the moment to a close, but they did not. They simply stepped back, weeping themselves, and witnessed with me the awesome power of God.

8

THE TRIAL

On the morning of my trial, it was unusually cold when I woke up. This was the day I would be able to confront my accusers and deal with matters, once and for all, in a court of law.

Max Siegel showed up early that morning with a suit and a tie and told me it would be advantageous for me to wear it. He did not want me to look like a thug. He told me that because he was from out of state, there was a strike against him and he did not need my attire or visible tattoos to hurt this case. Maybe I should have listened to him, but after what I had experienced the night before, I felt like Superman. I felt as though nothing could hinder what God had in store for me that day. I told him I would not wear the suit. I had known Max for a long time, and he knew me fairly well. But he was not happy with this choice. A look of disgust descended on his face as he told me to get ready and come on.

When we arrived at the courthouse in Monroe, we were led to a holding area. This was a small room on the lower level where those who would be on trial that day awaited their case number to be called.

"Do not be shocked if, after the prosecution rests, we don't call any witnesses," Max told me as we waited.

This caught me off guard. "You mean to tell me we will not get our chance to tell our side?"

"No, that's not the case," he said. "Many of the people I would have called to testify have been subpoenaed by the prosecution."

Max felt that the prosecution's case would only help and strengthen our case. He promised me that as he reexamined their witnesses, it would establish the foundation and proof that the charges against me had no merit.

The prosecution had subpoenaed Donya Wade, who had worked with me for twelve years. She was in charge of our ministry's Inner City Education Programs and wrote grants for our non-profit outreach. Other witnesses included Sergeant T. D. Miller, one of the detectives who arrested me on the night in question; my wife, Felice; and my sister Shelia Lakin.

James Benjamin Truesdale, my personal assistant, was also subpoenaed. James knew the ins and outs of the church's various outreach ministries and was knowledgeable about the neighborhood where I was arrested. To break it down, anybody who had anything to do with our church in that neighborhood—or who was affiliated with me in any form or fashion—would be sitting in the courtroom that day.

I sat in the holding area with Red Dog, Raheem, and the other guys who were on the Hill with me on that fateful night. We were all rather quiet. I spoke to Red Dog and Raheem. Red Dog told me that he was glad to see me. Raheem seemed to have an attitude. But after we chatted for a while, he seemed to ease up. "As long as we were selling dope, we didn't have any problems," Raheem said. "As soon as you came up and asked to pray, here come the cops."

I shook my head with a little grin and began to talk to Red Dog about his family, whom I knew well. He told me that his mother would be in the courtroom that day.

The prosecution had also subpoenaed a young man from P.O.D. 3200. I asked him why he was there, and he told me that he had been questioned about conversations he'd had with me in

3200. I began to shake my head in disgust because I'd never spoken to that young man. This did not discourage me; it encouraged me even more. Having had previous experience with the judicial system, and being an avid watcher of Court TV, I knew that the prosecution did not have a case. I had a pretty good feeling that I would be at home in my own chair later that evening, watching *The Moment of Truth* (a preaching program on our local cable access station).

The bailiff, a stern-looking officer whom I had seen before, entered the holding area. He called us all by name, stood us up, chained us together, and marched us upstairs to the courtroom.

One of the young men made the statement, "Somebody's going down today."

He and the guy at the end of the line began to laugh. The bailiff was not having it. He said, "We can do this two ways: Number one, we can walk up quietly and take our seats in the courtroom. Number two . . . Well, I'll keep that to myself, because I would rather show you than tell you." The authority in his voice was clear. He heard no more trash talking.

When we entered the courtroom, it was packed. I was fourth in line. I hadn't shaved or had a haircut in about a month. I was just ready to go home. I saw many people from the church, many from my family, and it felt good to pretend for a few moments that I was physically a free man. My mother sat in the back of the courtroom, and I was shocked to see her. Her name is Lizzie S. Kee. She had just gotten out of the hospital and seemed to be doing fine. Personally, I did not think that she needed to be there, but I was grateful that she was. She is the mother of sixteen children, and out of all of the junk that we put her through, she remained faithful to all of us. I nodded at her, and she gave me one of the best "It will be all right" looks that I had seen in a long time.

Elder Ben Truesdale escorted my mother. He took good care of her and would not allow any of the media to sit near her or ask her any questions. This was not a problem for my immediate family, for they were escorted by Officer Calvin Young and sat in the front of the courtroom.

I should insert here how moved I was when I saw Officer Young. You see, he is a North Carolina state policeman and a longtime friend who knew my vision to transform the inner city and had embraced it as his own. For Officer Young to be there with my family showed great character. He will never know how much his presence encouraged me.

I was disturbed a little because I had forgotten to tell my wife not to bring John-John to the courthouse. One of my brothers served time when I was a little boy, and it put an indelible print in my mind. I am thirty-nine years old and to this day I still remember everything about that experience. I remember the smell of the prison, the long wait to see him, the guards chaining and carrying him away. And I remember trying to feed him a potato chip before I left. I did not want this image in the mind of my son, nor did I want him to have to leave that room without me going with him. Still, I must admit that it was reassuring to see the smiling faces of all of my children—and my dear wife.

The bailiff shouted, "Everybody rise, the Honorable Judge S. D. Fritzgerald presiding."

We all stood, and in walked the judge. He was a white man, who looked to be about six feet tall and in his late fifties. He walked to his bench and sat down. His stare was most unusual. It appeared, through the small glasses that rested on his nose, that he had perfected the look of life plus twenty years. He had a face of stone. He gazed at me as though he had read a book that listed every sin I had committed from age twelve. I foolishly attempted to smile at him, but the feeling was obviously not mutual.

For some strange reason, I thought that there would be other cases prior to mine. I guess one of the reasons I thought that was because there was one young man in the lineup whom I didn't know. He was a dark-skinned brother with an afro. He looked familiar, but I couldn't recall where I'd seen him before.

When we sat down, the district attorney, a woman named

Vicky Harris, stood up and began the opening statements for the prosecution. I sat in disbelief at some of the things I was hearing. But I remained calm, looking directly at her. She looked rather young to be a D.A., but she spoke as if we were cousins. Every time she caught my eyes, she looked into them with a ball of fire as though she had a personal vendetta.

It's amazing how in the courtroom, every title that I'd ever gained was immediately stripped away. There was no "Minister," "Reverend," or "Pastor." It was humbling, but it gave credence to an old adage that I'd heard years ago: "I'd rather have an inward knowing than an outward showing." In other words, Harris began to rip up my physical man; nevertheless, I was able to smile because my spirit man stayed in check. I continued to stare right at her as she continued her opening statements. She said she would prove that on the night in question, "John Kee distributed an illegal, controlled substance to a group of men in a circle. The state will prove that this so-called preacher, in the last twenty years, has done nothing but poison this community." She stated that she would play videos and CDs where in my own words I testified that I indeed sold drugs in the Double Oaks community.

"He manipulated and deceived the people of Double Oaks by making them think that he was a good, honest, hardworking store clerk and part-time musician, when in fact he sold drugs and stolen goods, and physically assaulted some of those he was affiliated with," Harris added. "Some would ask the question, 'Why bring these things up now?' After twenty years as district attorney, I would answer, 'It was those things that he got away with that created the real monster that he is today. Those are the things he got away with that created his suspicious behavior in the Double Oaks community three months ago.'"

Harris then looked at the jury and said, "Ladies and gentlemen, what preacher leaves his house on a Saturday night at 9 P.M., drives over to the Double Oaks community, slows down, talks to prostitutes, parks his car, gets out, carries on conversations with them, picks up a known drug dealer, carries him to Bojangles

Restaurant, leaves Bojangles at approximately 10:45 and travels down to Double Oaks, slows down as if in heavy conversation, and then, ladies and gentlemen of the jury, goes to a pool hall at approximately 11 P.M., goes inside the pool hall, shakes everybody's hand, and when there is a known waiting list, jumps the line and plays pool immediately, brings one of his drug associates back down the street, and then goes and stands on a suspect hill where he has some type of drug hand-holding ceremony? Ladies and gentlemen of the jury, the city of Charlotte has a great reputation for banking, commerce, sports, and two of the top-ten private schools in the nation. And it is the degenerate scum like the defendant, Mr. John Kee, that we need to get rid of. There will be many who will come in and tell of his good deeds, how he is a pastor, a recording artist, an entrepreneur, and many other positive things. But ladies and gentlemen of the jury, I am not impressed. I submit to you that he is just a drug offender who has gotten away with it for twenty years. If we are going to clean up our streets, we have got to start somewhere. Thank you very much."

The courtroom was as quiet as a mouse. I was devastated. I saw my mother drop her head. Though I couldn't see my wife from where I was seated, I knew that she was hurting as well. I had never witnessed a face-to-face prosecution such as this. It was as though Harris was reading out of a John Grisham novel. She walked slowly back to her seat.

The jury was made up of two whites, both women, one man who appeared to be of Middle Eastern descent, five black men, and four black women. As Harris walked to her seat, it appeared that she stared at each one of them. They stared back solemnly.

The judge looked at my attorneys. "You may proceed," he said.

Max stood up and gave his opening statement. After such a riveting opener by the prosecution, I slumped in my seat slightly, worried that nothing could top the hold she had over the courtroom. Even though I knew everything she had said was wrong, it sounded quite convincing. I sat anxiously waiting to hear what Max would say. The first thing out of his mouth scared me out of my wits.

"Ladies and gentlemen of the jury, suppose I tell you that 90 percent of everything Ms. Harris said was true," Max began. "Suppose I tell you that Mr. Kee was indeed a drug dealer. He was not just a dealer, but he poisoned and infected the Double Oaks community for two and a half years. Yes, he did pose as a store clerk. But I'll go even further than the prosecution: He did not just pose as a local musician; he played in churches throughout this city, conducting choirs, doing concerts. He deceived many of the people who trusted him, doing things that were not expected of a young, honest citizen who was active in the church. Ladies and gentlemen of the jury, I will show you that this was not his choice but his course.

"My client, Mr. John Prince Kee, after twenty years of success in the business and musical arena, came back to Charlotte to proclaim his destiny. You will hear in the words of my client that he indeed was a troubled young adult who made many mistakes —many for which he never served a day of jail time. He could have gone on with his life, lived in a plush community, raised his kids, and never looked back. But ladies and gentlemen of the jury, I will prove through the cross-examination of the state's witnesses that my client is not the drug-dealing degenerate that the state has painted him to be.

"Yes, like few people I know, he will admit to a lot of things that happened in his past. But I promise you, before the end of this trial, you will meet a young man to be reckoned with. As far as our city and its reputation: yes, it is a mecca for banking, commerce, sports, and education, but along with that comes the hidden influx of prostitution and drugs. I will show you that this man, John P. Kee, has not only returned to our city to do what is right, but he has invested personal money so that our children might eat, our mothers might be sheltered, and our brothers might be given a second chance at life. We will show you with documented statistics how the crime rate has dropped since this man and his church have come into our community.

"As for the area of sports in our city, I find it to be a sad commentary that we can boast about our football, basketball, baseball, and hockey teams and not deal with the homelessness, hopelessness, neglect, and other frustrating issues that plague our city. As for the area of education, the defendant has purchased property and is in the process of building schools for the community. These schools will not just be accessed by his church population, but just like his summer enrichment programs, as well as his afterschool program, there are personal scholarships available for the families of the neighborhood.

"Ladies and gentlemen of the jury, we are not looking at a cancer in our community; we are looking at an antidote—a young man who has given countless dollars back to our community with no government assistance. It is very easy to call him a drug dealer and write him off as a thug when we are not willing to deal with the real issues that plague our community.

"Our strategy is simple. We believe that the state has no case and the only witnesses will be those whom my client encountered on that night. Pastor Kee is an honorable man in our community. Not only does he give back, unselfishly, but he is also willing to place himself in harm's way to get his message across. The two months and twenty seven days served for these charges were done without any complaints. This district attorney's office has used taxpayer money to create these charges. Let me recite them for you again: a felony possession to manufacture, sell, or possess with intent to sell a controlled substance. Ladies and gentlemen of the jury, we will show you that it is not the felony or the misdemeanor; it is his ministry that is respected in the Double Oaks community. Your Honor, our team is very pleased that you and the district attorney allowed this trial to be moved to Monroe. And we promise you, ladies and gentlemen of the jury, that this case will be tried in a courtroom and not in the media. As the judge has instructed you, I ask that you ignore the media hype surrounding this case. Because you have not been sequestered, I ask you to be fair, listen with your heart as well as with your head, hear the facts of the case, recognize it is all circumstantial, and let's let this good man go back home to his family, church, and hard work in the community. Thank you very much."

With that, Max took his seat. He not only spoke with confidence, but his opening statement left me with a new sense of resolve.

9

HEARING FROM THE OTHER SIDE

The state called its first witness, Detective T. D. Miller. As he walked to the witness stand, he looked over at me and nodded like he was my best friend. This was very interesting. Because of my inside connections, I discovered about one month ago that he had called the Spencer Drive jail facility to find out how I was doing. Officer Love informed me that this was not the first time, and on one occasion Detective Miller said to him personally, "Don't allow anything to happen to Pastor Kee." I never understood it, but even on the night of the arrest, during the interrogation, I noticed that after I shared with him my purpose for being in Double Oaks, he seemed to understand.

D. A. Harris told him to state his name and occupation. He responded in a low, raspy voice, "Detective T. D. Miller, special agent assigned to the Vice and Narcotics Unit."

Harris asked him how long he had been a part of this special force. "Approximately two years," Miller said. "I moved to Charlotte from New Jersey, worked three years in Robbery and Homicide, then joined the Vice and Narcotics team approximately two years ago."

Harris continued, "On April 9th, did you have occasion to question the defendant?"

"Yes, I did."

"Was he cooperative?"

"There was a time when he appeared to become frustrated and threatened to get up and walk out, but he did not," Miller said. "At first we thought that he was evading the questions by asking us questions. But after the first two hours, he calmed down and continued to drop his head in his hands, mumbling, 'I can't believe this.'"

Harris asked him a few questions about his partner, Detective Anthony Sloan. Then came the interesting part.

I found out, through Detective Miller's testimony, that they had followed me that evening from my house to the encounter with the prostitute, to Bojangles Restaurant, and then to the pool hall.

On cross-examination Max unearthed some interesting facts. "Did you have any knowledge of Mr. Kee before you moved to North Carolina?" he asked.

Miller dropped his head down, took a deep breath, held his head up, and said, "Yes, I did."

"What knowledge would you be referring to?"

Miller's response dropped my jaw. He told the jury that his brother-in-law was president of a gospel record label, Saval Records, in the state of New Jersey. This was not just any label. That label had pioneered some of the greatest traditional gospel music of all time. It was also a label that I had been signed to as a young writer. Miller stated that before becoming a police officer he had worked in the area of marketing for the label.

Max had a grin on his face, as though he'd known this information all along. "So you mean to tell me that on the night in question you already knew of this man and his ministry?"

"I did," Miller said.

The final question was simple: "Did you ever, at any time, see any drugs or drug paraphernalia in the hands of my client?"

"No."

Max looked at the judge, who did not appear to be paying attention to any of this, and said, "I have no further questions."

Harris jumped up and said, "I have one more question, Your Honor." The judge nodded his consent. "Detective Miller," she began, "did you witness this drug-dealing, hand-shaking ceremony that was going on at the top of the Hill?"

"I don't know what kind of ceremony it was, but I did witness them grabbing hands," Miller replied.

Harris said, "That's all, Your Honor," and gazed at me with a smirk before sitting down.

She then called her next witness, Officer Don Charles. After he was sworn in, he sat down. I had not seen him since the night I was arrested. He stood about 6'3" and approached the bench with an air of forced machismo, as though he sought to put fear in the heart of the courtroom. He actually caused me to laugh (under my breath, of course). As Harris began to question him, Officer Charles seemed not to remember all of the details of the night. He told the jury and the court that he remembered pulling his cruiser past the swimming pool in Double Oaks. He said he also witnessed something passing through the hands of everybody in the circle. As he got the go-ahead and approached the circle on foot, one of the young men fled. The district attorney asked if that young man was in the courtroom. He pointed over in our direction.

At that time, I found out the identity of the young man with the afro two seats down from me. He was Little Tony, the young man who had fled the scene, which made the officers very angry because they couldn't catch him.

Officer Charles went on to tell the details of the night as he remembered them. He said that when he approached me, it appeared I wanted to run but could not determine in which direction to go. At this point, I really wanted to tell Max something. I began to think about proper court procedure, and I wondered why I was still sitting in the box with the other defendants, during my own trial. I discovered that because they had moved the case to a local, rural county, the rules changed. I then asked the bailiff if it was possible for me to sit near my attorney. He approached the judge. They shared some type of a joke, and I was immediately taken over to the table. It was the first time I had a chance to really glimpse my family up close.

My wife, though as beautiful as ever, looked quite nervous. John-John looked like he wanted to come and sit on my lap. She-lia was asleep. Aieisha sat beside her, looking very attentive. Missing were Shannon, Chris, and Justin. I later found out that they were there, but because of the respect they have for their father and knowing that all of the charges were unfounded, they couldn't bear seeing me in chains, unshaven, and unable to reach out to them, so they sat outside the courtroom.

Harris asked Officer Charles if I had resisted arrest.

"He was somewhat cooperative."

"What do you mean 'somewhat'?" she said.

"While placing him under arrest, he continued to stop and interrupt during the reading of his rights, asking, 'What am I being charged with?'"

She asked Charles if he was familiar with the Double Oaks area, and he told her yes. He said he had been assigned to that area for about two years. Then out of his own mouth, of his own admission, he made a statement that I felt would help our case. "Other than this incident, within the past year there has been a huge decline in the area of crime in the Double Oaks community."

Harris, practically cutting him off, said, "No further questions."

I don't profess to be a mind reader, but I didn't think that was the answer she wanted to hear. According to Harris, the second half of his answer was not necessary.

Max got up and said, "Your Honor, I'll be brief." He asked the officer if he at any time had seen drugs in my hands. Officer Charles said no. Max asked him how long he had patrolled the Double Oaks area.

Charles seemed to get a little huffy and said, "I'll say it again. For about two years."

"How well do you know the area?" Max asked.

"Very well. About a year and a half ago, there were several stings set up in the area, and I served as arresting officer for many of the cases."

"Are you aware that my client built a church in that area approximately one year ago?"

"Yes," said Charles.

"Had you ever met him before?"

Officer Charles paused and said, "On one occasion there was a young man who had stolen a car during church service. Pastor Kee may not remember this, but I was the officer who came out to talk to the young man. It amazed me because in spite of this young man's indiscretions, the pastor and staff of this church still embraced him and just wanted the two officers and myself to let him know the severity of the crime he committed."

"What about that puzzled you?" Max asked.

Officer Charles said, "Well, when we ran a check on the young man, we discovered that he was already on probation for the same crime, and many times when you offend those who know you are on probation, they want to press charges. And on this particular day—"

District Attorney Harris jumped to her feet. "I object, Your Honor. This has nothing to do with this case."

The judge appeared to finally wake up. "Overruled," he announced. "You may finish your answer."

Charles continued, "On this particular Sunday evening, the pastor and staff refused to press charges but said that they would keep an eye on the young man because they believed he had a good heart."

"Let me ask you one more question," Max said. "Are you aware that since Pastor Kee and the New Life Fellowship Center have been in the Double Oaks community, the crime rate has diminished?"

"I can't say that it is because of Pastor Kee," Charles said. "But I can say that since they have been there and the trees have been cut down in the back of the project area, there has been less dealing, prostitution, and murder in the Double Oaks community."

Max said, "I have no further questions."

Harris jumped up again and said, "Officer Charles, one more question, please. Are you saying that Pastor Kee and his entourage are responsible for the calm in Double Oaks, or is it good law enforcement?"

"I believe it is a combination of all parties working together."

Again, that didn't seem to be the answer Harris was fishing for.

Judge Fritzgerald excused Charles from the stand and then instructed Harris to call her next witness.

To everyone's surprise, she called my wife to the stand. Felice stood up very slowly, looked at me, and nodded. She had been subpoenaed a month ago and had been told by our attorneys that she had the option to refrain from testifying against her husband. Being the woman of strength that she is, she chose to testify. After Felice was sworn in, Harris asked her where she was from— "Macon, Georgia"—and where she and I had met—"San Diego, California."

"Are you aware that your husband was a drug dealer?"

"What do you mean by *was?*" Felice asked. "As in *now*, or twenty years ago?"

"Just answer the question," Harris said.

Felice sighed and closed her eyes. This made me a bit nervous. I wondered why she would not just answer the question. I knew that she was frustrated because she could not clarify the manner in which her answer would be perceived.

Then Max jumped up and said, "I object, Your Honor. Is it possible for Attorney Harris to clarify her question?"

"Overruled," the judge said. "Just answer the question, Mrs. Kee."

Felice said yes.

Harris then asked, "Is it normal for your husband to leave on a Saturday night and go over to the area of the church before Sunday worship?"

"That has been a normal routine ever since I have known him," explained Felice. "In the summer months, he goes over and witnesses before studying at night."

"And what happens in the winter?"

"In the winter it is basically the same. He created a ministry about eight years ago called Pillow and Blanket. They pass out pillows and blankets in the winter and continue to witness to those who are homeless."

"Mrs. Kee, could you explain the Pillow and Blanket ministry a little more?"

Felice sighed. "Well, during the summer months, we collect old pillows and blankets from the households of attendees of our church. We clean them and restore them. When the weather drops below a certain temperature, we break up into groups of five or seven, carrying pillows, blankets, sandwiches, soup, and a small care package, and give them to the homeless."

"What's in this care package?" Harris said sarcastically.

"You know, things like—"

Harris interrupted, "Can you please speak up?"

"Toiletries."

"Is there a problem?" Harris teased. "Why don't you tell us specifically what's in the package?"

"No, there's no problem," said Felice, clearly irritated by her interrogator's attitude. "The packages contain soap, deodorant, toothpaste, toothbrushes, things of that nature."

Harris began to walk back to her seat. Under her breath she mumbled "care packages" in front of the jury. Then she turned before sitting and said cynically, "So you don't find it unusual that your husband is walking the street at night, hanging out in ceremonial circles, going to a pool hall, soliciting prostitutes—"

Max objected, "There is no evidence in this case that would support any soliciting of a prostitute."

Harris immediately apologized and rephrased the last part of her question. "You don't find it unusual that your husband has *conversations* with prostitutes."

"Absolutely not," Felice said. "Up until the time that we had our last child, I too was a part of the witness team that went out on the streets. This was not just an activity on Saturday night; it was a part of our ministry in the Double Oaks community."

After Harris sat, one of my attorneys, William Kee, stood and approached the witness stand. He asked my wife if she was OK. Felice nodded. He asked her, "Do you love your husband?"

"Yes."

"Have you ever, at any time, witnessed your husband involved in the illegal usage or selling of a controlled substance of any kind?"

"Absolutely not."

William turned to Judge Fritzgerald. "That is all that I have, Your Honor," he said.

Harris suddenly raised her hand. "I have just one more question for the witness, Your Honor," she said. "Are you with your husband twenty-four hours a day?"

"Not physically," Felice said with a quick smile.

Next, the state called Tim Raymond—a.k.a. Red Dog—to the stand. He seemed a bit nervous. Not the cool, calm, collected man I knew from the street. He sat down and stated his name.

Then something troubled me. For a few moments I felt very bad. Although I'd had nothing to do with this young man standing on the Hill that night, I felt totally responsible for him being on the stand. Because he was a witness for the state, I was certain he had made some sort of a deal with the prosecution. I was prepared for him to speak a lot of untruths. That's putting it mildly. I expected the brother to lie under oath. But, interestingly enough, that was not the case. He actually surprised me as well as District Attorney Harris. She became very agitated as Red Dog spoke because nothing about his answers condemned me. He became, as Harris put it, "a hostile witness." She pulled out his statement from April 9th, the morning in question, and began to ask him questions about that evening on the Hill.

His response to the statement made her furious. He said at

least seven times, "Madam Attorney, the night I gave that statement, I was so high, all I remember is Pastor Kee walking up the Hill and I being embarrassed because I had a joint in my hand. That is absolutely all I remember about that evening. The truth of the matter is, I just don't remember."

It seemed that the jury not only believed Red Dog, but they became increasingly annoyed by District Attorney Harris asking him the same questions over and over. I was very proud of Red Dog that day. Although his English was a little broken, his realness was unquestionably favored in the courtroom.

Harris asked one question in particular that really backfired on her. "How can you consider yourself a part of a ministry when, in fact, as you put it, you were smoking dope and too high to remember what took place?"

Red Dog turned to Judge Fritzgerald and asked him if he could answer the question without being interrupted by the attorney. The judge looked at him and said, "Give us your answer, Son."

Red Dog turned to the jury and said, "I was wrong. I was not only wrong; I was out of the will of God. As I reflect back on my situation, it was one of dumbest things I ever did. But while I was in jail, I had some time to think on what Pastor Kee was teachin' us. He told us that even though you find yourself in a slump, you ain't got to stay there. It takes a real man to stand up, admit he was wrong, and recognize that he ain't in bondage to that thang. I've had three months to think about it, and it ain't for the jury, Pastor Kee, or even the judge; my life is changed because of who God is in me."

Harris looked at him in total disbelief. Then she flashed a cynical smirk in the direction of the jury and said, "I have no further questions."

Max jumped up quickly and walked over near the jury box. "Can you tell the jury how long you've known Pastor Kee?" he asked Red Dog.

"Most of my life," he said.

It was approaching the lunch hour. Up until then the trial had moved fairly quickly. The judge interrupted Max and asked him how much longer he thought he would be.

"Just a few more questions, Your Honor," Max said. He turned back to Red Dog. "You stated earlier that you were embarrassed when you saw Pastor Kee. What did you mean by that?"

"I could tell that Pastor Kee was disappointed," Red Dog said.

Harris cut in, "I object, Your Honor. He cannot testify as to the state of mind of Pastor Kee."

"Sustained," said Fritzgerald.

Max apologized and instructed Red Dog just to tell the court what he felt during that moment. Red Dog said he was embarrassed but too high to control the situation. "I remember telling everybody, 'Let's just pray'. I wanted Pastor Kee to pray and get on about his business."

Max asked, "In the time that you've known Pastor Kee, have you ever known him to smoke, sell, or engage in any illegal drug activity?"

"No!" said Red Dog firmly.

Max had no further questions.

We recessed for lunch. The other prisoners and I were taken to a small holding area. Bag lunches had been prepared for us. Two bailiffs stood on each end of the room. We were not allowed to talk to one another. Lunch was a cold ham-and-cheese sandwich with a carton of milk and a piece of raisin bread. Believe it or not, it was actually one of the best lunches I had ever eaten.

Midway through the lunch, my attorneys entered the room with big smiles on their faces. One of my attorneys, Keith Cunningham, had begun to probe into the business dealings of Larry Martinez, one of the state's key witnesses. He was the real-estate agent who had purchased many of the homes in inner-city Charlotte. Martinez had formed a company called Laxley American. The company advertised with the slogan "Your Friendly Neighborhood Builder." Keith said that he had found out through a prominent city official that Martinez was being investigated. Laxley American had allegedly deceived hundreds of senior citizens and inner-city homeowners out of their personal property. The company would actually go into the inner city and promise homeowners that major renovations would be done on their houses for little or no money. The homeowners would then sign a contract full of dubious fine print. This scam was not the only thing that Martinez was being investigated for. Apparently, he was also being scrutinized because he had been hired by the city to be what some would call "the front man" for many suspicious dealings in the black community.

"In other words," Keith said, "the last thing that the D.A. needs in this case is to put Martinez on the stand and allow us to cross-examine him. They were bringing him into this case to testify that, as a pastor, you own property in the inner city, and that you were secretly meeting with the owners of Double Oaks to perhaps one day purchase it."

"Well, that is a desire of mine," I said. "I'd like to one day renovate the entire community."

Keith interrupted me. "Hold on, Pastor Kee," he said. "You are not on trial here; I am just giving you the information that has been uncovered."

"Yeah, calm down," William chimed in.

We all shared a laugh and Keith continued. He explained that this would poke a big hole in the state's case. The prosecution had based a lot of their claim on my alleged unlawful business practices in the community, and Martinez was their star witness. I personally was praying that Martinez would take the stand. I knew several families who had lost their homes to the "Friendly Neighborhood Builder."

I had known Larry Martinez since my days of hustling in the community. I will never forget the day that I saw him on the news. Local businessmen announced that they were coming together to clean up the inner city, and Larry was there front and center. I remember staring at the television in astonishment. There he was, smiling in front of the camera. He had on a brand-new suit and new front teeth. I must admit, I was proud of him when I first saw him. As he began to talk, I remember sitting up and saying to myself, "What a blessing," because if anybody knew about the inner workings of the Charlotte streets, it was Larry.

Did I mention that Larry had been a partner of mine in the Charlotte underground? We had crossed paths several times, and it was not a marriage made in heaven. In my early days of being questioned by the police, it was Larry who tried to turn me in so that he could rule my territory. This, of course, had nothing to do with my opinion of him one way or the other. I was actually happy when it appeared Larry was doing something positive. I figured if God could change me, he could definitely change him.

It was not until he began to talk about incorporating questionable business practices into his "Clean Up Our City Campaign" that I became concerned. So I would frequent the public meetings he convened at local community centers and challenge the ethics of his proposed plans. They all hated to see me coming. But I was very concerned that the principles of a program that we had started in our church to build up and stabilize inner-city communities, by teaching basic economic principles, would be prostituted and irreparably damaged by this man and his organization. Needless to say, I was not surprised when I learned that he would be testifying against me. But I was concerned because, with our past history, there was no telling what he would say or do. The truth was, if he could get John P. Kee behind bars, it would be a lot easier for him to realize his disingenuous goals in the Double Oaks community.

Finally, it was time to go back to the courtroom. Max told me that the next witness to be called would possibly be Wanda Wilburn. I had noticed her sitting near the back of the courtroom. It was painful to watch her because this was a woman whom I had loved like a sister. She appeared to have lost a lot of weight. Her son, Quincy, was sitting beside her. I nodded and he nodded back, as if to say hello. I was sure this was going to be a very interesting afternoon.

Before the jury returned, there was a brief sidebar with the judge and attorneys. It concerned the testimony of Tony and what could and could not be asked in the presence of the jury. The district attorney was still fighting to get the cocaine that was seized the night of the arrest introduced into the trial. My attorneys fought it tooth and nail because the cocaine was not found in my possession.

The jury was finally permitted to return to the courtroom. As predicted, the prosecution called Wanda to the stand. District Attorney Harris asked her a lot of personal background questions—where she was born, where she had been raised, where she worked. This took about twenty minutes. Then she asked about her son.

Wanda said that she was a single mother. She told of how Quincy and I had become good friends. She trusted her son in my company until she began to see things that concerned her. "He began to skip school and sneak out late at night," she said. "The truth of the matter is, the only stable thing about him was that he had to see Pastor Kee. So I began to ask myself what kind of influence Pastor Kee was having on this child. As far as I could see, Quincy was headed in the wrong direction. Yet his role model was still in the picture."

"Is this man that you speak of present in the courtroom today?" Harris said.

"Yes, he is," Wanda said. "He is sitting right over there at the table, with the orange shirt on."

"Let the record state that she is pointing to the defendant, Mr. John Kee." Harris looked back at Wanda and asked her, "Has your son ever been arrested?"

"Yes."

"Do you remember the charges?"

Wanda looked at me and said, "Possession with intent to sell."

"Did your son tell you that he got the drugs from Pastor Kee?"

Keith sprang to his feet. "I object, Your Honor. This is hearsay," he said.

"Sustained," ruled Judge Fritzgerald.

"Let me rephrase my question," Harris said. "Did your son at any time tell you where he got his drugs?"

Keith jumped up again. "I object, Your Honor."

"Sustained," said the judge.

Harris continued, "Ms. Wilburn, did you feel that the relationship Mr. Kee shared with your son was good or bad?"

Wanda paused for a moment before answering. "At first it was one of the most positive things I had ever experienced," she finally said. "Quincy started to do well in school; he was hanging in a more positive environment. Then it appeared that something just cracked. He started to disrespect me and everything was about 'Pastor Kee.' Then came the music and the pictures."

"What do you mean, 'pictures'?" Harris asked.

"There were always posters of Pastor Kee's CD covers. To tell you the truth, I just got tired of hearing that man's name."

Max reached over and whispered something into Keith's ear, and they smiled. I wanted to tell Max that I was the one on trial—if he had some good news, I needed to hear it. After a few more unflattering comments about me, D.A. Harris completed her questioning.

The judge looked over at our table and said, "You may cross."

Keith Cunningham stood up, buttoning his jacket. "Thank you, Your Honor," he said. He gave Wanda a rather stern look, as though he had figured something out from her earlier testimony. "You told this jury you were pleased at first with the relationship between your son and Pastor Kee."

"Yes, I was," Wanda said.

"Is it true that you actually shared with many of your friends that Pastor Kee was a perfect role model and father figure for your son?"

She drew a deep breath. "I have said that on occasion."

"Ms. Wilburn, earlier the district attorney asked you where you were employed. Where are you employed again?"

She dropped her eyes and slowly said, "Lance."

Keith looked at her sharply. "Mrs. Wilburn, hold your head up, look at the jury, and tell them where you are employed. And remember that you are under oath."

"I am unemployed," she said.

There was seemingly a collective gasp from everyone in the courtroom. Then a brief silence.

I was a little surprised by this sequence of questions. Although I was heartbroken that Wanda would testify falsely against me, I never wished anything bad to befall her. But she had perjured herself. Regretfully, she would have to face the repercussions of it after the trial had ended.

"Mrs. Wilburn, is it true that in the fall of 1999 the division of Lance Corporation that you worked in was downsized and your job was terminated?"

"Yes," she answered as tears spilled from her eyes.

Keith locked his hands behind his back and began to walk in front of the jury, like a stereotypical lawyer on a TV show. "Mrs. Wilburn, you come into this courtroom today to testify that my client has been somewhat of a thorn in your flesh, when in fact if it had not been for my client, you would have lost everything. Mrs. Wilburn, do you remember a meeting with Pastor Kee, in his office, in December of 1999?"

"Yes."

"Could you tell the jury the nature of the meeting?"

She paused for about twenty seconds and then tearfully began to speak. "I was about to lose it all and he had really been there for my son and me."

Cunningham brought her a box of Kleenex. She wiped her nose and continued. "I have made some bad choices—not only with my finances, but also with friends that I started to hang out with. At the meeting, Pastor Kee told me that the only way he would help me would be if I cleaned up my act. I personally felt that because of the relationship he had had with my son, his helping me should not have been determined by my actions or the people I involved myself with."

My attorney asked her in a soft, confiding voice, as though no one was in the courtroom but him and her, "Is this the real reason you are in court today?"

D.A. Harris quickly rose. "I object, Your Honor."

"Sustained," declared Fritzgerald.

"Let me rephrase," Keith said. "Out of all the great things this man has done for you, why accuse him of your son's drug involvement?"

Wanda began to weep loudly. She looked over at me and said, "You were not there. We needed you. I not only lost my house, but I lost my car. I lost everything. You can't walk into the lives of these kids and then just leave them."

I stared directly back into her eyes with a gentle, sympathetic gaze. I knew that I had done all that I could do and that cocaine had ripped her household apart. She continued to cry and scream uncontrollably, even after Keith completed his cross-examination. The judge signaled the bailiff to remove her from the stand and then from the courtroom.

Still, she continued to shout, "You could've helped me!" It was clear to the jury, as well as to everyone in the courtroom, that her anger against me had nothing to do with her son. The pain and delusion of addiction was speaking loudly and clearly.

As she was led out of the courtroom, her son stood beside her and nodded at me as if to say, "It is going to be OK." I really believed in Quincy. I was convinced that he would not only break away from drugs and a reckless lifestyle but that one day he would pursue God's purpose for his life.

I glanced over at the D.A.'s table. They appeared to be scrambling. Whatever they had planned to get out of Wanda on the stand, it had not come to pass.

Judge Fritzgerald asked the prosecution to call its next witness.

Harris and company called Sheila Dobbins. Dobbins was a detention officer who worked at the Spencer Drive jail facility where I had been locked up. As she took the stand, I looked at Max and Keith. Max said, "Don't worry about it."

It wasn't that I was worried; I just did not know what she would bring to the prosecution's case against me.

Harris asked Dobbins for her name and occupation and then got down to the business at hand. "Officer Dobbins, while the defendant was incarcerated at Spencer Drive, did you ever escort him to meet with any outside visitors or attorneys?"

"Yes," Dobbins said.

"How many times?"

"Approximately five or six."

"Did you have occasion to escort him to a meeting with a man named"—Harris looked down at her notes and said slowly —"Elder Ben Truesdale?"

"Yes, I did," Dobbins said.

At this point, a little back story may be necessary. While I was locked up, an article appeared in a local paper with the headline PREACHER CONFESSES TO JAILER. This story claimed that I confessed to a jailer, telling her that I was a part of a drug ring and spoke in a code that only she and an unknown visitor could understand. The article reported that I said, "We need to move the rock, and the rock should be moved slowly so that no one will get hurt." Because this was one of many stories, we shrugged it off and treated it as though it was what it was—tabloid-style garbage. It was only during the trial that I discovered that the guard mentioned in the article was Sheila Dobbins.

Now, on the witness stand, Dobbins testified that on the day in question, I and a visitor—Ben Truesdale—were speaking in code about rock cocaine. She said, "They continued to talk about this rock, that rock, and how they would move it slowly." According to Dobbins, because she was street smart, having been raised in the projects of Warren, Ohio, she knew exactly what we were talking about.

D.A. Harris asked her repeatedly, "Are you sure this is what you heard?"

"Yes," Dobbins responded.

When Max began the cross-examination, he asked Dobbins,

"Did Pastor Kee and Mr. Truesdale ever use the words *rock* and *cocaine* together?"

"No," she said, "but I was raised in the streets. I know these things."

Max cut her off. "Ma'am, I simply asked you a question: Did you ever hear the words *rock cocaine?*"

"No."

"So if I submit to you that they were talking about a rock in one's front yard, would you say that I am telling the truth?"

She shrugged her shoulders sarcastically, and then said, "They were talking about rock cocaine."

"I have no further questions, Your Honor."

That was all Max said. And frankly, I was upset. I vividly remembered the conversation that Ben and I had had. Max and I had discussed it several times, so when he didn't pursue the subject further with Dobbins, I was perplexed. "Why didn't you clear that up?" I asked him as he took his seat.

"I am the attorney," he told me firmly. "You have to trust me. They are going to call Ben Truesdale to the stand later, and I will clear it up then."

I was concerned because they never said Ben's name. They referred to the person I had the conversation with as an unknown subject, as though it was some high-notched drug dealer from another state. I was not comfortable with this. The jurors, who had seemed to warm up to the notion of my innocence, appeared to relapse into their stone-cold demeanors. I took a deep breath, sighed, and sat back in my chair. *Lord, it is in Your hands,* I said silently.

The prosecution's next witness was my parishioner and staff member Donya Wade. To this day I still don't understand why Donya was put on the stand. Absolutely nothing she said served to help the state's case. Donya, a talented singer who directed the education programs at my church, handled the awkward situation extremely well. D.A. Harris was unable to unearth any incriminating evidence from her. However, during cross-examination, my attorneys came close to doing damage where the prosecution wished they could have.

Max got up and briskly walked toward the witness stand. "Donya Lea Wade," he said confidently, "have you ever seen or witnessed any drugs in the possession of Pastor Kee?"

Donya slowly raised her head. Just as I prepared for her to answer, "No, never," she shocked the courtroom and Max when she said, "Yes, I have."

You could hear a pin drop. Everyone gasped at the same time. The temperature in the room seemed to drop several degrees. Chatter began throughout the courthouse.

The judge repeatedly slammed his gavel. "Order in the court."

Max's voice appeared to break. "Excuse me," he said, "what do you mean?"

Judge Fritzgerald, who had appeared indifferent to the whole proceedings thus far, removed his glasses and sat straight up in his chair. With a sharp southern drawl, he said, "Ma'am, you may answer the question."

"I have witnessed rock cocaine in Pastor Kee's possession," Donya said.

At about this time it felt as though my vital signs had all shut down. I had known Donya for years and for the life of me I could not remember one time when there had been any form of any drug in my possession during that period, let alone at a time when Donya was present.

Then she told the full story. "It was late one Friday night. We were having a street revival, and Pastor Kee began to preach about the power of deliverance. The service had gone on for five days and had attracted a cross-section of young and old. Pastor Kee preached a poignant message that night entitled 'I Escaped Without Stinking.' He based his sermon on the story of Shadrach, Meshach, and Abednego from the Old Testament book of Daniel. That night, he taught that regardless of your past, you could receive another chance and come out on the other side as a new person, cleansed of the sins that used to drag you down. The

91

message was so powerful that the altar call was like none other. Hundreds of people flocked forward.

"Pastor Kee stated that many would surrender things that were in their hearts, but more specifically, there were some in the tent that night who needed to surrender physical idols as well. There were things they had brought in the tent that night on their physical body that they would need to give up."

The courtroom listened in rapt silence as Donya recounted the story. But the most shocking part was yet to come. She went on to say that two young men had walked to the altar—two men who in any other situation would have scared her witless. "By their outward appearance, you would have never thought they would enter any kind of evangelistic event. But being the church stenographer, I had a seat at the front of the tent and could clearly see their faces. They were weeping uncontrollably." Donya's voice began to crack. Clearly, something about that night had made an indelible imprint on her soul.

She continued, "Many people who came forward that night threw cigarettes, pills, syringes, and other drug paraphernalia on the altar. But those two guys went in their pockets and handed Pastor Kee seven or eight bags of what I later learned was crack cocaine. They were laying it down at the altar."

District Attorney Harris jumped up. "I object," she said. "Can we approach the bench, Your Honor?"

All of the attorneys approached the judge's bench. I could not tell what they were saying, but Donya appeared totally shocked. They seemed to bicker, and whatever they were arguing about had Donya's eyes frozen wide open. I later found out that D.A. Harris felt that Donya's testimony was beyond the scope, but Judge Fritzgerald ruled in favor of the defense and said that this was the state's witness and they should have been better prepared for what she could possibly say. Fritzgerald sent everyone back to their seats, and Donya finished her story.

"Pastor Kee took the bags of crack cocaine and gave them to Calvin Young, a security officer in the church. Brother Young was not just a security officer; he was a local police officer. He and two of the men from the security team carried the cocaine into the men's restroom inside the church and flushed it."

Donya turned away from the jury, looked District Attorney Harris right in her eyes, and said, "So, when you ask me if I have ever seen drugs in Pastor Kee's possession, my answer is yes, I have, but not with the intent to use or to sell. It was demonstrated clearly to me that night that his sole intention was and is to clean up the inner-city communities."

Once again, Harris sprang to her feet. "I object, Your Honor," she said. "This is no more than a witness's opinion."

"Overruled," Fritzgerald asserted again. "You opened the door; let Ms. Wade finish answering the question."

Max took a deep breath, looked over at the prosecution's table, and said, "That will be all, Your Honor."

Donya, with tears in her eyes, stood up and slowly walked back to her seat. The judge instructed her that she could be called again as a witness.

10

A TRUE WARRIOR

The state called their next witness, Mr. James Benjamin
Truesdale. Ben had supported my ministry for years. In the
past five years, he had become one of my closest friends. Ben had
a personal testimony that would blow your socks off. He had
lived with diabetes most of his life and on a day-to-day basis had
to endure kidney dialysis treatments. But he never complained.
Ben was one whom I not only trusted and drew strength from,
but oftentimes I would ask him jokingly, "Are you sure that we
didn't have the same daddy?" And he would laugh and tell me,
"Of course we do."

In hindsight, I really believe that because the state was not
able to call Larry Martinez they would call Ben Truesdale, to
prove that our ministry owned more than just property in and
around the Double Oaks area. Ben not only worked with me at
the church he was one of my chief negotiators in all of my business dealings. He had knowledge of everything I was involved in.
I sat in peace, for I knew there had been no illegal practices in
any of our businesses. But I was concerned because I could tell
that the D.A. was getting a little frustrated. It appeared that Ms.

Harris had stuck her hand in a pot of gold and continued to pull out sour grapes and lemons.

As Ben approached the witness stand, I was proud to be his friend. You see, Ben and I shared another joke. I have never been a stylish dresser, but I received a lot of nice outfits from clothiers who wanted me to promote their clothes nationally. When these clothiers offered to send me free items, I would always give them Ben's size. So, when Ben stepped out, he was always exquisitely dressed from head to toe. There is a slang term, *representin'*, and I want you to know, on this day, Ben was doing just that. He had on a charcoal gray suit, a pair of black Martin Dele's shoes, a white custom-made shirt, and a Kenneth Cole tie.

From her chair, D.A. Harris asked Ben about an eighteen-acre plot that I had supposedly secretly purchased for personal gain. I sat in my seat wondering where in the world the district attorney got her information and why it wasn't checked or verified before the trial.

When asked about the eighteen acres, Ben responded calmly. "When we first began looking at the property," he said, "Pastor Kee wanted to purchase it, but I, along with a few more of the staffers, decided it would be in our best interest to partner with the county and develop this property for the community."

Harris looked at him and said sarcastically, "Mr. Truesdale, can you be honest with the court today? Isn't it a fact that Pastor Kee wanted this property to build private homes and then sell them for personal gain?"

"Absolutely not," Ben said.

She continued as if she did not hear his answer. "Isn't it a fact, Mr. Truesdale, that you all entered into an agreement with the city with the intention of building homes, stores, and other business complexes to increase the revenue of this so-called pastor?"

Ben laughed and began to answer, but before he could finish his statement, Harris shouted, "Mr. Truesdale, isn't this true?"

"I object, Your Honor!" Max yelled. "The prosecution is badgering the witness."

"Sustained," said Fritzgerald. "You have asked that question twice, Ms. Harris. Can you move on to the next question?"

"Yes, Your Honor." Harris turned back to Ben. "Mr. Truesdale, could you explain to me this Adopt a Family program that you are the co-director of?"

"Yes, I can," answered Ben. "Pastor Kee developed a program that would target single-family homes, and the rules are pretty simple. If you are a single parent, working a steady job, and there is no spouse in the home, and a need is clearly established, Adopt a Family will step in and help without asking a lot of questions."

"How would you determine who qualifies for this particular program?" Harris asked.

"Sometimes when the situation is not urgent, potential recipients come in and fill out an application. Then, with our limited resources, we try to verify as much of the information as we possibly can and then we assist the family." Ben now spoke in a measured rhythm, as though he expected Harris to interrupt him. "But many times, in emergency situations, we immediately attend to the situation."

Harris leaned back with her glasses on her nose and said, "OK, Mr. Truesdale, could you tell me the hour in which many of these emergencies take place?"

"Normally, it is late at night. Many times it is after midnight."

"Would Pastor Kee assign certain people to attend to these matters?"

"Sometimes," said Ben, "but most of the time he would actually do it himself."

A smug expression registered on Harris's face. "That's what concerns me," she said. "After subpoenaing the bank records, I discovered that many of these checks were written after midnight. I find it strange, Mr. Truesdale, that one would shop and spend thousands of dollars after midnight. Were you ever present during these purchases?"

"Because of my health condition, many times I didn't go late nights. But I own a truck and oftentimes assist them by delivering or bringing the goods back to the church."

"The goods?" Harris said cynically.

"The groceries," Ben added.

"So, Mr. Truesdale, is it your testimony today that you all have an operation that you say purchases and buys things for families, and all of these activities take place after 11 P.M.?"

"Yes, we do have such a program," Ben said. "And the majority of the outreach does take place late at night and early in the morning."

Max rose again. "Your Honor, I object. This has absolutely nothing to do with the charges."

Harris responded, "Your Honor, we are showing that the late-night behavior of the night in question is characteristic of Mr. Kee's behavior."

Fritzgerald said, "Overruled."

Harris continued, "Mr. Truesdale, why are these deliveries made at night?"

Ben sat up with a little smile on his face. "I have been waiting for you to ask me that question."

The judge did not like this prefacing statement. "Mr. Truesdale, just answer the question without unnecessary remarks," he admonished.

Ben nodded apologetically. "When we go into any public place during the day, many times we cannot move as fast because of Pastor Kee's professional status. People often stop and want to greet him or get his autograph. It never bothers him. He is always willing to stop and shake hands, sign an autograph, or just offer a warm smile. So, because the purchases are so large and we have to move as swiftly as we can, we started years ago buying items late at night and then delivering at that time. And you ought to see the faces of the kids and the parents when we show up at night with the bags. It is as though—"

"That will be all, Mr. Truesdale," Harris said.

Max walked over to Ben on cross-examination and asked, "Mr. Truesdale, how often are you at the church during the week?"

"Every day. I get there at noon and normally I am the last one there. I lock up."

"Are you there alone?"

"No. One of our church slogans is 'The Church Without Walls,' and there is always something going on at New Life."

"Mr. Truesdale, this Adopt a Family program that you co-chair, is that the only program within your church?" Max asked.

"No, there are approximately fifty active programs in our church."

"Does Pastor Kee participate in these programs as well?"

"Absolutely," Ben said with a smile.

"In the area of your role as chief negotiator for the church, were the eighteen acres of land that Ms. Harris questioned you about negotiated and purchased for the private and personal use of Mr. Kee?"

"Absolutely not," Ben said. "First of all—"

Harris was clearly not happy with the direction of this questioning. "I object!" she shouted.

Ben interrupted her and said, "Your Honor, can I please explain my answer?"

The judge banged the gavel on his desk and said, "Order, now." Then he said, "Overruled," and told Ben that he could explain his answer.

"Although we wanted to purchase the property," Ben said, "the city never agreed to it. The only other option was a partnership with the county. We would then maintain a park on the south end of the property. We went back and forth for six months and came up with a lease agreement that worked for the county as well as the church."

Max said, "Were there ever any plans to build private homes or any other types of real estate on this property?"

"I remember in one meeting Pastor Kee discussed the concept of doing transitional housing, but we already had a facility beside that property that could have been utilized for that purpose. That was the only time that was discussed."

"So, Mr. Truesdale, you and the county came up with an agreement."

Ben answered, "Yes we did."

"Could you share with the court what it was?"

"A portion of the property will be used for parking, and we have decided to put three parks on the property." He added, "Double Oaks had been promised many things by the city, so we were happy that we were able to resolve this matter, build our new church, and service the community."

Max said, "So, Mr. Truesdale, on an average, how many hours do you think you spend around Pastor Kee?"

Ben looked back and closed his eyes as though he was calculating. "From Sunday to Saturday, well over seventy hours."

"Mr. Truesdale," Max continued, "I want to touch a very sensitive area. The D.A. brought up an issue with Pastor Kee and an unnamed subject who had a conversation with him in the jail. Did you ever visit Pastor Kee at the jail?"

"Several times."

"In any of your visits, did you ever meet Detention Officer Dobbins?"

"Yes, I did."

"Is she in the courtroom today, and if she is, could you point to her?"

Dobbins was a very muscular lady who stood about 6'2". In short, she could not be missed. Ben pointed directly at her.

Max said, "Did you have a conversation with Pastor Kee about rock cocaine?"

Ben dropped his head. Those who didn't know him may have thought that he was getting ready to confess something that would have me locked up for years to come. But I knew that anytime Ben dropped his head, the words that followed would be words of wisdom and truth. And that was the case this time too. "Pastor Kee and I did discuss a rock that day," Ben said. "When we built the first facility there were trees that blocked the view of our church. Pastor Kee did not stop until every one of those trees had been removed except for three. After the trees had been removed, the prostitutes had nowhere to hide, the drug dealers had nowhere to scheme, and the crack users had nowhere to smoke."

As Ben spoke, Harris appeared increasingly uncomfortable. She began to talk to the other attorneys at her table. I could tell that they didn't have a real conversation. It was more like a pep talk between colleagues. They just wanted to show their solidarity and that they were still on top of their game.

Ben continued, "After the woods had been removed, there was an old rock down behind the property, up against the brick wall that divided our property from Highway 77. There were those who wanted the rock removed, chiseled, and taken off of the property. But I told Pastor Kee that we were not moving that rock. If anything, I wanted the rock placed at the front of the property. We argued about that old rock for months. Finally, I had a bulldozer come in, pick up that rock, and bring it to the edge of the property."

"Excuse me, Mr. Truesdale," Max interrupted. "When Officer Dobbins testified that she heard you two stating, 'Move the rock slowly so no one would be hurt,' what did that mean?"

"The rock was very large," Ben said, "and Pastor Kee was concerned that if the men of the church moved the rock it would roll back down the hill and hurt someone. So we agreed that if we moved the rock, it would have to be professionally done. On three occasions it was stated by him and me that we should be cautious, take our time, and do it right."

"When you spoke with Pastor Kee in the presence of Officer Dobbins, were you whispering or speaking in normal volume?"

At this point, Ben's agitation with the situation began to slip through the cracks. "We never whispered," he said. "We had no reason to whisper. We were having a conversation about a huge rock that is sitting in front of our church right now." Then he added, "There was something about that rock that gave me a peace."

It was as though Ben was testifying, not in the sense of testifying on trial, but the kind you'd hear from a traveling evangelist at a midweek revival service. He said, "You see, I am no negotiator or business consultant by trade. I was at a point in my life when I felt like it was all over for me, and this man that you have on trial today gave me an opportunity to live again. In areas of business he respected what I said, and much of what I brought to the table was good old-fashioned common sense. We would be in meetings with high-ranking officials, builders, agents, and attorneys, and no decision would be made unless I had the final say. I know that he is just a man; he is not Jesus. But I thank God that He gave me a brother like John Kee." He dropped his head and for the first time, I saw a tear roll down his face.

This was a man whose body, although frail because of his physical condition, would always appear strong and in control. But never before had I seen him so vulnerable and unable to contain his emotions.

"Are you OK?" Max asked softly.

"Please let me finish," Ben insisted. "When we discussed that rock, Officer Dobbins heard us, and we did not bite our tongues. We talked about the church, we talked about reaching people, and to tell you the truth, I talked about myself." His voice was shaking now with each word. "Every night when most of you go home, you can lie down and go to sleep. But in my case, it's very different. At the age of twelve, I was diagnosed with diabetes. I learned something very early about real life. The days go a lot faster when you don't complain." He shrugged his shoulders as if to hold back tears. "I stand today because of my foundation in God. When I wake up in the morning, the first thing out of my mouth is 'Thank You, Lord, for another day.'

"You see, that rock meant a great deal to me. Every day that I would pass by that rock, on my way into the church, I knew it meant I had a chance to touch somebody else's life with my testimony. It is not just about a church, Pastor Kee, or the building of schools; it is all about having a strong foundation. When I see that old rock, it just reminds me that I do have something to stand on. So yes, Officer Dobbins heard us arguing about moving a rock, but it wasn't about moving rock cocaine throughout a community; it was moving that rock to the edge of the property that represented my strength and stability."

"That will be all," Max said.

Ben got up and slowly walked back to his seat. He looked over at me. "It's time to go home," he said as moved to the back of the courtroom to sit beside my mother.

I smiled because I knew that I was ready to go home. This turned out to be a powerful moment, not just in the trial, but also in the lives of everybody who was in the courtroom that day. As I looked around, there was not a dry eye in the place—even Harris seemed to be moved. The judge, though still stone-faced, had been touched deeply, and he announced a fifteen-minute recess. Although Ben had gotten down from the stand and the jury had been ushered away, my friend's testimony still reverberated in the courtroom.

11

WRAP IT UP

After the recess, we reassembled in the courtroom and the state called Raheem to the stand.

D.A. Harris asked Raheem, "Do you know the defendant?"

"Yes."

She then asked, "Have you on any occasion ever seen Pastor Kee supply, use, or distribute drugs in any form?"

He said, "Yes, ma'am," and tried to explain.

Harris cut him off, saying, "Just answer the question, Mr. Blackmon."

Raheem became visibly angry at the D.A.'s heavy-handed approach, but he held his composure. Harris asked him questions concerning that infamous night on the Hill and his personal involvement. Raheem was very forthright and honest. He said, "I had been drinking up until 5:30 that evening, and by the time the bust took place, I was too high to gather my faculties."

That tickled me because I had known Raheem for a long time and had never heard him use the word *faculties*. I guess that was something he picked up while in jail.

She asked him, "Do you remember praying in a circle?"

He looked at me and said, "John, I don't mean no disrespect."

Harris interrupted him and said, "You are not testifying to Mr. Kee; you are testifying to the court and to the jury."

"My bad," Raheem said. He looked at her and said, "I just don't remember."

By now, Harris was becoming even more agitated. She went to her table and pulled Raheem's earlier statement and told him to read a few paragraphs to refresh his memory. After Raheem read his statement, Harris asked, "Does that refresh your memory?"

He looked up at her and said, "Ma'am, I can read this one, I can read every statement on your table, but as far as that night is concerned, my recollection will be based on what I read today."

"Are you telling me that you don't remember the night, even now?"

Max jumped up with an objection. "Your Honor, the witness has stated time and time again that he does not remember."

The judge said, "Sustained. Ask another question."

Harris said, "Have you ever witnessed Mr. Kee at any time selling any type of drug or controlled substance?"

Raheem paused slightly, then said, "Yes I have."

As he tried to explain himself, Harris cut him off. "Just answer the questions as I ask you, sir. Have you ever witnessed him using any drug or controlled substance?"

Raheem dropped his head and slowly said, "Yes, I have."

Harris fell back in her chair and said, "No further questions."

Now it was our turn. Keith Cunningham walked over to the witness stand and looked Raheem in the eye. "The last two questions that you were asked by the D.A. concerning drug sale and drug use, could you tell this court when that took place?"

Raheem said, "It had to be between 1979 and 1980, because in 1981 he left the game."

"Could you explain to the jury what you mean by 'left the game'?" Keith said.

"He come up from them streets to live a better life."

"So are you suggesting that the behavior the D.A. asked you about happened twenty-two years ago?"

"Yes."

Keith said, "No further questions."

The judge looked at the prosecution. "Will that be all?"

Harris stood up and said, "Your Honor, I have one last question." She asked Raheem, "Do you remember the location that you witnessed Mr. Kee selling drugs?"

"Yes, ma'am," Raheem said.

She asked, "Could you tell the jury where that was?"

"Yes," he said. "It was over on the Hill on Statesville Avenue."

Harris said, "The Hill, the Hill. Are you referring to the same place where this incident in question took place?"

"Yes, ma'am."

She said, "The state rests, Your Honor."

We retired for the day.

12

IT'S MY TIME

We entered the courtroom at about five minutes before nine o'clock the next morning. This was the day the defense would have their time to tell what took place. Max stood up and called his first witness. "I would like to call Deidre Carter to the stand," he said. As she walked down the aisle, she looked familiar. But like many of the other witnesses, I wondered what she had to offer this case.

As she approached, her face became more familiar, but I could not pinpoint from where I knew her. And then it hit me. Deidre Carter was the prostitute I encountered on April 8th, the Saturday night prior to the early Sunday morning on which I was arrested.

She looked poised and professional. Max told me he had a surprise, but I thought he said the witness was a "he," not a "she." He asked her to state her name and occupation.

She sat straight up with broad shoulders and said, "Deidre Carter." She had gotten a job with a local phone service and she said, "I am part-time vice-president of a program in our church called WAIM."

I sat straight up in my chair, not just because she had a job, but because WAIM was a program that I had developed in our church. WAIM stands for "Women Anointed In Motion." It was a program designed to empower women for ministry inside and outside the church. Before I was arrested, I had no knowledge of this young lady being a part of the program. The young lady I had appointed director over the program was Shelby Talton. She was a firm believer in giving others a chance. So in my mind I just imagined Deidre going in with her testimony and Shelby immediately giving her a position.

As Max questioned Deidre, I learned that she had attended our church the Sunday morning after my arrest and had found out about it through Elder Truesdale. Apparently, he had stood up in the church and told all of the saints what had happened to me the night before. Deidre said that she was very sure of the conversation I had with her that night, and because of my words and example she surrendered her life.

This enraged District Attorney Harris. I could tell this was not the testimony that she wanted to hear.

Through his examination of Deidre, Max was also able to allow the jurors more information about the church and the programs that had been envisioned and implemented in the Double Oaks community.

It would be an understatement to say that Harris was not prepared for this witness. She had gathered a lot of information about Deidre's past. But it did not seem to bother Deidre at all. She sat tall and admitted to some things that would have caused any skeptic to question the validity of her conversion. There was arrest after arrest, a couple of convictions—not to mention she was still on parole as we sat in the courtroom that day.

After Harris finished, Max stood up and called his second witness. When I looked up I could not believe it. Dressed in a suit and tie was Duey Wright. This was the young man whom I had a chance to minister to before I went to jail. I had not heard from him since then. However, Ben had told me that he had also come to church the Sunday after my arrest. Duey was clearly a changed man. He had gained at least ten pounds, and I had a hard time remembering what he had looked like before. As he sat down, I was overjoyed that he was there.

Duey testified that on the night in question, he rode with me to get something to eat and stated that I also accompanied him to the pool hall. He said, "After playing the game, I promised Pastor Kee that I would be in church the next Sunday." He turned out to be a key witness for our defense, because he testified that on several weekends he witnessed me ministering to the young and old in Double Oaks. He testified that he had lived in the community for twenty-four years. He had seen its rise and fall, but he believed that the New Life Fellowship Center was the greatest thing to ever happen to Double Oaks. He made mention of several deaths that took place right before our moving in. But now it appeared that the crime had ceased—or at least slowed down considerably. He said that his children were being educated at our school and that it was "a blessing to be able to drop your kids off and know that they would come home with knowledge and true understanding."

Out of all the great things Duey said, I was not prepared for his next statement. I thought that he came to court dressed like he was dressed just to be there for me. But I found out this was greater than me. He testified that as a result of the evening we spent together, when he read the papers and heard the stories, all he could think about was the food and the fellowship that we had had prior to my arrest. He said, "Yes, he entered the pool hall but I know without a doubt in my mind, it was all ministry."

"How do you know that it was ministry?" Max asked him.

"Here is a preacher who does not take a salary. Why else would he be in a pool hall evangelizing people who don't even have jobs?" Duey said. "Many churches want paying customers. This ghetto preacher was not concerned about my money; he was concerned about me getting my act together." Then Duey turned to me and said, "So today, as I sit in this courtroom, I can say that I saw his going to jail as a sacrifice, because I know what took place that night and that man is no drug dealer. From that night to this morning, I reevaluated myself and changed my ways. I have been attending his church ever since he was locked up, and I am happy that I can testify that I am not the same man."

On her cross-examination, Harris stood up and immediately tried to undermine his credibility. "So you are not the same man?"

"No, I am not," Duey said.

"Is it true that in 1981 you were convicted of larceny and grand theft? And you also served three years in the state correctional facility?"

He calmly answered, "Yes, ma'am."

"Is it true that in 1986, you were arrested on spousal abuse?"

"Yes, I was."

"In that same year, are you the Mr. Wright who was arrested in an armed robbery attempt at First Commercial Bank on Broward Street?"

"That was me," Duey said with a wide smile.

"Are you the Mr. Wright who in 1993 was charged with breaking and entering a Family Dollar warehouse and served three more years in the state's correctional facility?"

"Absolutely."

"Mr. Wright, are you the same man who in 1998 was stopped on Interstate 85 and arrested for having possession of a stolen vehicle?"

"That was me."

Harris shook her head. "Not only does it appear that you are a career criminal," she said, "but you seem to be happy about it."

Max interjected, "I object, Your Honor. Counsel is making statements, not asking questions."

Harris apologized and then went at Duey from another angle. "Mr. Wright, with you admitting to all of these charges, how is it that we can believe anything you say?"

Duey looked right into her eyes. "That is the great part of my testimony today," he said. "I have found out that through the blood of Jesus, I am not guilty." Then he looked at the jury. "I am truly a changed man."

That testimony alone made my day. I did not know what was to come. I knew that I would be next, but I went on the stand convinced more than ever that God received the glory out of that evening that I was arrested for praying on the Hill.

Max called my name. As I walked up to the stand, I looked back at my wife. She nodded as though she was praying for me. My eyes immediately connected with my mother's. She gave me a gentle smile. Ben, strong and steady, looked like a general in the Army. Without raising a hand, he saluted me through his silent gaze of respect and encouragement. I even saw my friend and business partner Regi Miner standing in the back. Although I knew he was feeling anguish over what I had experienced those last months, I could still see a grin on his face. It was a grin of faith. He knew me and he knew my ministry. There was not a doubt in his mind that the Lord would take care of me.

I sat on the stand and Max asked me only two questions. First, "On the night in question, what were your intentions as you approached that group on the Hill?"

"I love what I do," I told him. "I went there with no other purpose than to pray with them and encourage them to find a better life."

Second, "In the last twenty years, have you ever sold, used, or supplied drugs?

"No, I have not," I said.

"Are you sure?" Max probed.

"Absolutely."

D.A. Harris's line of questioning was not quite as succinct. "So, Mr. Kee," she said, "is it fair to say that you have been clean for twenty years?"

"Twenty-one years, four months, and three days," I said.

"How can you be so sure?" she asked.

"Deliverance is something that is not only special to me, but in my area of ministry it is something that I promote. There is no way I can promote deliverance unless I know my own history."

"OK," Harris said. "Let's talk about your life before this time period of cleanliness. Did you sell, distribute, or use drugs at that time?"

I believe my answer to that question startled her. I looked her square in the face and said, "I absolutely did." I then looked at the judge and asked if I could explain my answer.

He said, "Go ahead, Mr. Kee."

"I not only sold, but I distributed drugs throughout the Charlotte community. I saw the Double Oaks neighborhood slowly rip apart. After I surrendered my life to the Lord, it was my dream to come back to that neighborhood and create opportunities for the young and give stability and peace to the old so that we might restore our community and rid it of the ills of inner-city violence and hopelessness."

Harris turned and looked at the jury. "So when we speak of this Saturday night, April 8th, is it your testimony to this jury that your sole intention for walking on that hill was to pray?"

"Absolutely," I said.

She was not done. "Explain to the jury why it appeared that something was being passed around the circle."

Max jumped up. "I object, Your Honor. That is speculation."

"Rephrase the question, Ms. Harris," the judge said.

"Mr. Kee, did you pass something into the hands of the young men in the circle?"

Before I could get my answer out, she got louder and said, "Mr. Kee, do you remember Officer Don Charles's testimony?"

I told her I did.

"Do you remember that he said as he approached the scene, he noticed that some of the young men were putting things in their pockets?"

"I do remember him saying that."

"Do you have an explanation for that?"

"Yes, ma'am. It is real simple," I said. "It took me a few moments to get them to a place where they would pray with me, and I honestly believe they agreed to do it just so I would leave. So as I asked them all to join hands, whatever was in their hands they had to place in their pockets."

She laughed sarcastically. "So is it your testimony to the court,

Mr. Kee, that they placed things in their pockets before prayer and you did not give it to them?"

"I absolutely did not."

She then asked how long I had known Duey Wright. "About twenty years," I told her.

"Would you call him a close friend, an acquaintance? How would you describe your relationship with him?"

"A close friend," I said.

She looked at her notes and then asked, "Are you aware of his criminal record?"

"Yes, I am."

"Yet you called him a close friend." She shook her head. "That just doesn't make sense. It appears that you are living two lives." She went on for approximately thirty minutes trying to discredit me, asking me if I knew every drug-dealing thug in Mecklenburg County. I probably knew eighty percent of the names she mentioned. Every time I answered yes, she looked back at the jury as if she had scored a point. Just as she was about to close, she asked me where I lived.

I gave her my address.

"You love the community so much that you live about twenty-four miles away," she scoffed.

"I did purchase a home for my family," I told her. "But my ministry, my heart, is the Double Oaks community."

She looked at me and frowned. "Mr. Kee, could you please just answer the question that I asked you."

She pulled straws for about fifteen more minutes until she finally grew too frustrated with my responses. I sighed with relief when she told the judge she had no more questions.

Max immediately rose from his seat. "I have one more question, Your Honor." Max turned to me and asked, "Have you ever gone up on that hill before?"

"Numerous times," I said. "I have shared over and over again that this is the highlight of my ministry. Being able to go to those brothers, right when they were in the act, and let them know that in Christ there is a better life."

The judge then recessed for lunch. Before allowing the jurors out, he informed them that the attorneys would be ready for closing arguments that afternoon.

13

CLOSING ARGUMENTS

As we all walked back into the courtroom, the place had a different aura about it. It was very quiet, and I sensed that District Attorney Harris was confident that her closing argument would bring the house down. She looked over at me and smiled. This was definitely a first. Harris had been stone-faced from day one, so now either she thought she was going to crush me, or she was glad that it was all over. Either way, I could tell her fire was still burning. She stood up, straightened her jacket, and walked over to the jury. She scanned their faces carefully, searching for a connection with each juror. With a wide smile on her face, she began her speech.

"Good afternoon, ladies and gentlemen of the jury. We are here today to make a difference—a difference in the lives of the people who are seated in this courtroom. But it goes beyond that, ladies and gentlemen. Your decision today will affect the lives of your loved ones; people like you and me, your children and my children; people who do an honest day's work every day of their lives; people who want their children to be able to go outside in their yards or on the streets and know that they are safe. Charlotte, North Carolina, is one of the fastest-growing cities in this country. It has taken over twenty years to clean up the garbage that has settled here. And you, ladies and gentlemen, can be the vehicle of true change, right here, today, in this very courtroom.

"You see, on April the 8th, a man by the name of John Prince Kee—" Harris looked at me and shrugged, with a level of disdain I had not previously seen in her eyes—"a man who is a pastor of the New Life Fellowship Center, a church in Charlotte's inner city, was arrested for possession to manufacture, sell, or possess with the intent to sell a controlled substance. How do we know this? He was caught in the act. You see, ladies and gentlemen, through-out the entire night of April 8th, and throughout much of his spare time, as we have clearly seen in this trial, he keeps compa-ny with well-known drug offenders, lawbreakers, and deviants. These same people have sat before you, albeit dressed in their Sunday's finest, still having a criminal record. Many of them have been locked up or arrested on the very same charges. Let's ask ourselves this question: Were they dressed in their Sunday's best on the night in question? No, of course not. They were living their lives, out on the streets, on the so-called Hill—exchanging, selling, and using drugs. They were participating in criminal drug activity that continues to take lives and destroy communities. If we continue to slap these people on the wrist, we will continue to see the downfall of this city and this country. So, don't let the new clothes fool you; that is a common tactic used by defense teams in cases such as this."

Harris began pacing in front of the jury box. "Ladies and gen-tlemen, it stops here. You can make the difference. Here we have a man, Mr. John Prince Kee. He is wealthy. He has influence over others, maintains a large conglomerate of employees, and is a pas-tor. He even built his church, the New Life Fellowship Center, in the heart of Charlotte's inner city—Double Oaks, a neighborhood that our local news labeled one of the most dangerous in which to live. He has also admitted to being involved with drugs in his past and has quite a lengthy police record; yet he dresses up and calls himself a pastor. Does that make sense to you?"

This was funny to me because, if there is one thing I don't do, it's dress up. I often teach on Sundays in a warm-up suit. This has been a tactic that I use to keep the attention off of John P. Kee and on the Word of God. It allows people to know that they can come and worship as they are.

But I understood that lawyers specialized in painting pictures with common stereotypes, especially during their closing arguments. Harris was just doing her job. She continued, "Here is a pastor who socializes with half-dressed prostitutes, picks up street people, and spends a Saturday night in the local pool hall. It just doesn't make sense, does it? A pastor? In my experiences—and I am sure even in your experiences—you have never met a pastor or a decent, honest, hardworking man who maintains such a circumference of negative, criminal activity and constituents. It simply doesn't make sense."

Harris walked toward the defense table and then turned back to the jurors. "Ladies and gentlemen, let's address another outlandish issue. When and where have you ever seen a group of young black men stand in public, in an area known and documented for drug traffic, holding hands?" Harris looked into each of their eyes, almost forcing them to make direct eye contact with her.

To be honest, she looked smug. My flesh immediately wanted retribution, but my spirit hurt for this woman. I immediately began to pray that something about this trial would open her eyes and that she would begin to see past her personal pain and cynicism and see the possibility that God could heal and transform broken people.

But at that moment, she was on a mission to take me down. "Ladies and gentlemen, here is a man who has the means, the charisma, and the power to obtain and move drugs in a neighborhood that struggles to survive. He is like a predator, preying on innocent families and their children, people with no hope. And yet he drives Cadillacs, luxury SUVs, and even rides around in his very own limousine. And what is his defense? A hand-holding ritual? Evangelism? Jurors, it is insulting to present such a defense to intelligent, hardworking, honest men and women such as yourselves." She stared at me as if to guide the jurors' eyes in my direction. "It just doesn't make sense," she said. "Let's let history speak for itself, but let's not let history repeat itself. You hold the power in your hands to do something strong and decent for this community. Don't let watered-down words, emotions, or Sunday's best beguile or deceive you. It is your responsibility and your duty to find Mr. John Prince Kee guilty of all charges. Let's take one more criminal off the streets so that others will have a decent chance at an honest life. That is all we are asking. No more pats on the back. It stops here, with you, with each of us. Thank you very much for your attention." With that, Harris returned to her seat.

When she sat down, there appeared to be confusion in the court. For a few seconds there was nothing said or done. While she gave her closing arguments, the judge seemed to be writing something down and he seemed concerned with a matter other than what was going on in the courtroom. After a while, he slowly held his head up and said, "The court will take a fifteen-minute recess."

As the jurors exited, not a single one looked in our direction. I looked at Max. His eyes beamed with confidence. Without saying a single word, he told me not to worry. The bailiff escorted me out. To be honest, it was perhaps the longest fifteen minutes of my life. I was ready for it to be over with.

After the brief intermission, I was brought back to the courtroom. My three attorneys were engaged in lively conversation. Their next move, it seemed, was a bit of posturing for the jury. They reached over and shook my hand, as though we had already won the case.

Finally, it was time for our closing argument. Max had a large stack of note cards in his hands. He stood, looked at the jury, and laid the cards on the table. Slowly he removed his glasses and laid them on top of the notes, as if to say he was abandoning his prepared statement. If it didn't work for the jury, it worked for me. His message: This speech would come directly from the heart.

"Good afternoon, ladies and gentlemen of the jury," Max began. "I stand here today wearing three hats. I wear the first hat as a sworn officer of the court; the second, as a defense attorney; and the third, as a friend of a man I've known for many years. I could go on and on about our personal relationship—who he is and what he means to me but that is not why we are here. We are here today because the state wants you to believe that this man, my client, Pastor John P. Kee, is not an upstanding, law-abiding citizen but a drug-running, Cadillac-driving, late-night pool-playing, twenty-rolling, big-baller preacher who has deceived and poisoned the community.

"They want you to believe that on the night in question, he left his home at 9 P.M. and traveled to the Double Oaks neighborhood in order to socialize with prostitutes and drug dealers, and to sell drugs himself. But the state did not march one witness into this courtroom who could testify that Mr. Kee sold, attempted to sell, used, or was seen with any drugs or drug paraphernalia. Their entire case is founded on two men who say they saw John Kee pass drugs in some ceremonial circle."

Max continued, looking from juror to juror. "If there was ever a case filled with circumstantial evidence, it is the case that has been presented before this court. Let's look back at his actions that evening. He goes by a friend's house to check on him, a Mr. Grady Seigel. He does not sell Grady any drugs. And though Mr. Seigel was on the state's list to testify, you didn't hear from him. Now, I submit to you there was a reason for that. The reason is very simple—Mr. Seigel has absolutely nothing negative to say about Mr. Kee.

"What about the prostitute, Deidre Carter? Although the prosecution did everything in their power to rip her apart, she stood firm, admitting her wrong and declaring that because of that evening her life has been changed. Now, she would have been a great candidate for the state's case except she too started to attend the church and is vice-president of WAIM. Now she is able to touch the lives of many who were walking the street like she was, because of this man who saw a need to witness to her and touch her life.

"And what about Mr. Duey Wright? He didn't come into the courtroom and say that Mr. Kee passed him drugs. And you have got to remember one thing: He is the last person Mr. Kee talked to before he walked up on that hill. Ladies and gentlemen of the jury, what does Mr. Duey Wright say? He says that because of that encounter—that brief encounter that showed him that somebody genuinely cared about him—he got his life in order. So the prosecution takes twenty minutes to throw his past in your face. Just to prove that Pastor Kee associates himself with the misfits of our society. What a case! Mr. Wright didn't lie; he admitted to all of his wrongdoing, just like Ms. Deidre Carter and my client, Mr. Kee."

Max shook his head in disgust. "So do we convict this man because of his association with bad people, or do we look at the real picture and see that these people who have been deemed bad, deviant, and career criminals have gained a new lease on life?"

He put his hand on the rail in front of the jury and leaned forward to look at them. "I sat in my chambers and prepared for four days the closing argument of a lifetime," Max said. "I structured it so that it would not only make sense but be able to rip the state's case apart from start to finish. But as I sat there, it became clear to me that this case is not about win or lose; it is about effecting change. I simply ask you this question: How could my client be charged with trafficking when in fact, by their own admission, those he came into contact with before being arrested have totally turned their lives around?

"I am sure that every one of you sitting on this jury may deem my client's actions as not becoming of the normal orthodox preacher. What preacher would leave the comfort of his home and literally go to the streets to minister to those who are lost?

Pastor Kee holds strong to his faith, and he believes that God called him to go and touch the hearts of those who will never come into a four-wall structure. Let's look at the Double Oaks community. You heard Ms. Harris say that our own local news labeled the Double Oaks community one of the most dangerous places in Charlotte to live. I submit to you, ladies and gentlemen of the jury, that since this pastor and this ministry have moved to that neighborhood, the crime element has almost disappeared. Like any neighborhood, whether in the suburbs or in the inner city, there will always be some criminal activity. But instead of going after Pastor Kee and making him the scapegoat, we should be grateful that a man of his stature didn't turn and walk away, but returned after twenty years to offer hope to this community.

"You heard from Ben Truesdale. Ben's testimony is imperative to us because Ben knows the true nature of my client. Ben's testimony unquestionably shows us that instead of demeaning or judging those whom some might call deviant, my client was willing to give them a chance. I could stand up here all day, but the burden is not on me and it's not on Mr. Kee. The burden is on the state to prove its case. And I submit to you now that they have not done that.

"I agree with the prosecution's statement that it is now time to clean up our streets. But I know and you know that, instead of locking this man away—away from his family, away from his church, away from the people who respect and love him—it is time for us to send him back into that community. For the truth of the matter is, he will ultimately go, touch, and help to change the lives of those individuals whom you and I would never greet, meet, or come into contact with.

"Finally, ladies and gentlemen, I want to talk about motive. As we look at his financial statements, at his accomplishments, it just does not seem to fit. First, he could have sent somebody else to do his dirty work. And second, they were holding hands. What sense would it make for a pastor with such a wide following to be caught nickeling and diming on a hill? If he were a drug dealer, wouldn't he know how to play the game better than that? By his own admission, he sold drugs twenty years ago. He would have sent somebody else to do it for him."

Max turned and looked at the spectators in the courtroom as if his outrage had finally peaked. "I'm disgusted that nobody on this prosecution team thought to deal with motive," he shouted. "Ladies and gentlemen, let's place him at the scene of the alleged crime. It was called some type of hand-holding ritual. This is when it becomes hilarious. When has anybody ever known black men in an inner city to get high and stand in public and hold hands? In knowing my client personally, there was one argument we always had. I have shared with him on numerous occasions that he must find someone to help him with this late-night street ministry. But he always told me, 'It's my calling. You may never understand.'"

Max began to pace back and forth in front of the jury. Then he looked up and said, "The truth of the matter is, I didn't understand until we came to trial. I knew of the millions of lives he touched with his music, but this trial put it all into perspective. He would indubitably give up the millions to touch the hundreds of lives that he is able to physically see in the Double Oaks community." He turned to the prosecution's table. "Ms. Harris," he said, "you stated on many occasions throughout the trial, 'It just desn't make sense.' Well, maybe not to you—and ladies and gentlemen of the jury, maybe not even to me. But it is clear now, through the testimonies of all these who have come through this courtroom for the prosecution and for the defense, that something spoken through my client is allowing him to inspire and encourage these people on the street. He doesn't choose anybody to go for him, for he believes in his mind that he was chosen to go himself.

"There's just one more thing. What the detectives and the officers saw that night on the Hill was not some ceremonial drug exhibition but my client helping others to get their lives on track.

My client's sole purpose for being on the Hill that night was to pray for the souls of the people in that circle."

Max took a deep breath. "Ladies and gentlemen, Charlotte has several problems in the inner-city community—drugs, teen violence, carjackings, bank robberies, and the list goes on. I believe that there are a lot of solutions—some that work and some that will not. As you begin to deliberate, I want you to remember one thing: Mr. Kee is sitting in a holding cell, and he is one of the solutions to our city's problems. Don't lock this man away for the sake of saying we are doing something to help the city. Come back into this courtroom with the only verdict that should be found, and that is 'Not guilty.'"

14

THE VERDICT

The time we had all been anticipating seemed to approach faster and faster. The judge sat up straight, there was a brief sidebar, and then he gave instructions. The jury listened quietly. There was an older juror sitting in the front left corner. After Ben's testimony she began to weep, and from then on she occasionally looked at me and nodded. There was a white woman in the back row who seemed very nervous and agitated by the whole ordeal. Most of those who testified seemed to scare her.

To tell the truth, you really couldn't read this jury. I don't know if any jury can be read. But if my freedom depended solely on this jury's mood, for a few seconds I felt like I was in trouble. They finished gathering their instructions from the judge and then the bailiff took them off to deliberate my fate. I was given an option to either go into the back waiting area or sit at the defense table. This was not normal procedure. But we were right in the middle of the country in Monroe, North Carolina, and they seemed to make up their own rules as the trial went on. I chose to remain in the courtroom.

The jury had only been out for one hour when the bailiff came over and whispered something into Max's ear. They decided for safety reasons that it would be better for me to be held in the back. I didn't understand that because I didn't feel threatened in any way. After being back there for about an hour and a half, the bailiff knocked on the door of this small room where I sat with my attorneys and said, "We have a verdict."

They brought me out to the courtroom where I stood quietly beside my attorney. The jury walked in slowly. The foreman was a man who stood just under six feet tall. He had a small grin on his face. I couldn't judge if the grin was for me or against me. And then, like sweet music to my ears, he said these words: "We the jury find the defendant, Mr. John Prince Kee, not guilty of all charges." The courtroom erupted in mayhem. Everybody seemed to be rejoicing —everybody except for the prosecutors and the detectives.

After the verdict was read, the bailiff came over and took the shackles off of my feet. They took my family and me into a small room on the right side of the courtroom. When we entered the room, I noticed that my mother, my attorneys, and Elder Ben Truesdale had entered also. We all joined hands and began to pray and thank God. Ben led the prayer and it was as though he too had been locked up. "Dear Lord, out of all we've gone through, You blessed us, and we will bless Your name," he said. There wasn't a dry eye in the room. The presence of the Lord permeated the place.

There was a small sporting-goods store just across the street from the courthouse. My cousin William said he had sent Brian Smart, one of my personal security guards, across the street to pick me up something to wear out of the courthouse since he had no idea that the jury would come back with a verdict as fast as they had.

Max told me I would have to make a statement to the media. It was about 6:30 P.M., and the truth of the matter was that I was ready to go home. Before I could answer I felt a hand touch my shoulder. I knew it was my mother. She told me that she believed in me and that through all that had transpired, her faith never wavered. She leaned down and kissed me on my forehead and told me she was proud of me.

With my hand clinched tightly in the hand of my wife, I could not hold back my tears any longer. I began to weep uncontrollably. Back in the day, to shed tears in front of your loved ones was considered a sign of weakness. On that day I knew it was a sign of relief and joy that God was faithful.

About that time, Brian Smart entered the room with a bag. The logo on the bag read Happy Hills Sporting Goods. In the bag was a pair of black sweats, a blue sports shirt with a striped green collar, some Converse tennis shoes, and a blue baseball cap. The hat was much needed because I hadn't had a haircut in about a month. Brian told me that there was a dress shirt, slacks, a shaving kit, and other personal items on the way to the courthouse. He said these items were purchased just so that I would have something to wear when I faced the media. I stood up and looked out the window. What I saw moved me. There were about a hundred parents and kids from the Double Oaks community standing in front of the courthouse with signs declaring, "Free Pastor Kee!"

Now I would have to deal with the media—the media that had not, in my opinion, treated me fairly. It seemed that the moment I was locked up, all of my adversaries came out of the woodwork and that every day there was a negative story on the evening news or in the local paper.

I told my wife to ignore the stories. That was the same day that she called me and told me there was an outrageous report on the national news—"Gospel Artist Admits to Being Part of Drug Ring." I was an avid watcher and reader of the news. I believed that everything would be recorded and reported fairly. Not so. Where this case was concerned, there were enough stories for everyone to add his personal spin. So, I frankly had no intentions of interacting with the media.

I asked Max, "Is there any way I could wait and give a statement the following Sunday at my church?"

He told me that would be fine but that it was imperative that I give some sort of statement on that day. People from our church and fans of my music would eventually go home, he said, but the media would hang around for the long haul. "Look, you don't have to preach a sermon," Max said. "Just remember there were some loyal supporters throughout this whole ordeal who would love to hear from you. You can give any statement you want to give at your church on Sunday, but today you have to say thank you."

Max and I had a strange relationship. Though we often butted heads, he respected me and I respected him. He had been my personal attorney since he graduated from college. In all the years of our relationship, personal and professional, he'd never charged me a nickel. So, I decided to listen to him. I went into a small bath area and changed into the clothing that Brian gave me. I got dressed in a hurry. On my way out, I figured out that we were in a room adjacent to the judge's chambers.

To my surprise, Judge Fritzgerald walked out of his chambers into the waiting area. He shook my hand and told me to be encouraged and keep doing what I was doing. He complimented all of those who had testified from our church and told me it was a blessing to have committed Christian people around me. He rubbed John-John's head gently and shook the rest of the kids' hands and exited the room. I looked into my wife's eyes and said, "Our God is truly amazing."

Ben had been one of my confidants and protectors for a long time. If I stayed at the church too long or he felt that I needed rest, he would always say, "Pastor Kee, it's time to get out of here." He looked up and said, "Pastor Kee, let's see the media, because it's time to go." He looked at the bailiff and said, "Are you supposed to be leading us? If so, come on."

We all shared a brief laugh. We were all taken to a room that resembled a banquet hall, where there were three long rows of press people. Before taking our seats, I allowed the attorneys to go in and answer all of the legal questions. Attorney Max Siegel stood and said, "We will not be taking questions today. We will be taking questions at three o'clock Sunday evening at Pastor

Kee's church."

The attorneys also informed the media that I would simply be making a statement that day. After twenty or so minutes of Q & A with the attorneys, it was my turn to address the press conference. Officer Calvin Young escorted my family and me to the main table. The cameras were flashing, and people were shouting all kinds of questions: "What will you do now?" "Were you ever in danger while in jail?" "Will you continue pastoring in the neighborhood?"

I ignored the barrage of questions and stuck to our plan to make a brief statement. My comments were simple and to the point. "I want to thank God for my friends and family who supported me." As I was speaking, the emotions of the whole ordeal finally caught up to me. I paused, regained my composure, and then said, "But most of all, I want to thank God for Jesus, who died to free me. I'm a grateful man today. That's all I have to say."

Felice sat to my left. As I looked into her eyes, I could see that she was fighting back tears. I leaned over and kissed her. I was so happy to be sitting there with my family, knowing that I would soon be joining them back at our home. I grabbed John-John, who looked at me as though he was never going to let me out of his sight. Chris had been very quiet. The whole ordeal, I would discover, had a deep, personal effect on him. Aieisha's pretty face was filled with a look of relief that the nightmare was finally over. Shannon, whom we called our little prophetess, looked as confident and unflappable as ever. Justin was happy just to leave the courthouse. Tredell looked as though he couldn't care less. Just give him something to eat. John-John, in his cute broken English, smiled at me, looked at his mother, and said, "Is Daddy going home with us?"

Felice leaned over and kissed him. "Yes, baby, Daddy's going home."

15

NOT GUILTY

I was seated in the back of a stretch limousine, surrounded by my wife and kids. After three months as a prisoner, I was free —and I was going home. But before we went home, I needed to do something. I told the driver that I needed him to take me somewhere. I asked him to take me to Double Oaks. I needed to stop by our church. I longed to go into the temple, lift my hands, and worship.

As we approached the church, there were many cars parked in the lot. This was not unusual, because we sponsored a Pro Am basketball team and many of the games were held on Saturday evenings at our church. I didn't want to interrupt the game. I knew that if I walked inside the church, it would cause a disturbance. But there was such a need and a desire to lift up my hands in that temple. Nothing could have stopped me that day.

We drove by the old rock that Ben Truesdale had insisted we preserve. I'm glad he did. Out of all I had gone through, for the first time I agreed with Ben—the rock represented stability. Tears welled in my eyes as we approached the front of the building. I clenched my fists, pulled myself together, and got out of the car.

My wife grabbed my hand. John-John grabbed the other hand, the other kids followed, and we walked into the building.

When I opened the door, I was shocked to see scores of people standing and cheering, "Surprise!" How they pulled this off I will never know. Many of the people had parked on the other side of the church. I had held it together in good fashion for that entire day, but all of a sudden my emotions got the best of me. I wept uncontrollably. I had spent all of those days behind bars, feeling like there were only a few standing with me. But that was not the case. Suddenly, I realized just how many men and women, boys and girls had been faithfully praying for me daily.

I walked into the sanctuary and the choir began to sing. "Holy Lamb, Thou art worthy / Worthy of all the praise / Holy Lamb, Thou art worthy / Oh how we worship Your name."

I'll never be able to describe the fulfillment that I felt on that day. A spirit of worship spread throughout the building and ignited our souls.

After the choir had sung, my business partner, Regi Miner, walked to the podium. He gave honor to God and thanked everybody for showing up on such short notice. I later learned that as soon as I was pronounced "not guilty," Regi and Ben had the secretary of the church call every partaker of our fellowship and invite them to our church for our homecoming celebration.

Regi thanked the church for their prayers and encouraged them that if ever there was a time for us to press forward and to ratchet up our mission to live out the Gospel and bring deliverance to captive souls, it was now. With a tear in his eye, he told me that he loved me and vowed to not only stand behind me but to stand with me.

The crowd erupted in applause. Next, Ben came to the podium. He thanked God for a day that he would always remember. Then he charged the people of God to square their shoulders and hold their heads high, because "we have a unique ministry that was on target for an hour such as this." He exhorted them to follow my lead and become catalysts for change in the community. "We have a job to do," Ben said. "And if ever there was a time to embrace those who are lost, to teach those who are unlearned, to encourage those who are forgotten, and to present Jesus to those who are unsaved—it is now."

Ben's voice began to break a little as he led us all in prayer. Afterward, he called me to the front. We embraced, and I turned toward the crowd. I hadn't stood in this position for months, and it felt a little awkward.

The people were applauding. I looked to my right and there were Do-Wright and Big D holding a banner that said, WELCOME HOME. I looked to my left and was amazed to see Detective T. D. Miller with his family. He gave me a thumbs-up sign, as if to say, "Congratulations." There were at least 150 kids standing around the altar with smiles wider than the ones they usually flashed when the ice cream truck rolled up. I thanked them for their prayers and support during my period of crisis. I quoted Romans 5:1, "Therefore being justified by faith, we have peace with God through our Lord Jesus Christ" (KJV).

Then, inspired by the support of my people and moved by God's Holy Spirit, the words just started to flow. "Today we stand here and give God total praise for every prayer, every song, every tear, every letter, every lie, and every truth. It all worked together for the good. Out of it all I stand today with a testimony of undeniable deliverance. I made a personal decision to stay in that jail until my trial date. I know that it was hard on my family, but they stood by me. I am sure it caused some of my church family pain and put them in a position of having to defend their pastor. But Romans 5:1 says it all. The word *justified* means acquitted. The Bible tells us that because of our faith, we are not only deemed 'not guilty,' but we also have peace with God. This peace means that we are 'not at war with God.' In these past few months I have gained a peace about my relationship with God that cannot be defined by words alone. Rather, it is made manifest through my praise.

"I am not bitter. I believe in my heart that because of you who

are standing here today"—I glanced over at Detective Miller—
"something good came out of this trial. For years I testified that
God would never leave me. And it was in the dark hour—when
I felt like I was crazy, when I felt as though what I stood for mat-
tered to no one else—that God not only comforted my spirit but
strengthened me to know I could make it another day. You must
understand: I knew I was innocent. Yet there was still a transfor-
mation that happened inside those walls that caused me to grow
spiritually. Romans 8 became my best friend. For the days I wanted to condemn myself, I recognized that condemnation was not
a part of God's plan for those who walk in His Spirit. On the days
I felt like giving up, the Spirit quickened my mortal body and put
me back in my place. On the toughest days, I recited Romans
8:18, 'The sufferings of this present time are not worthy to be
compared with the glory which shall be revealed in us' (NKJV).
This reminded me that God would get the glory out of every
week, day, minute, and second of my ordeal.

"I sat in the courtroom, being judged by my peers, merely
because my definition of ministry had gone past the four-wall
structures of what we call church. But there were two verses that
I quoted daily: Romans 8:28—'And we know that all things work
together for good to those that love God, to those who are the
called according to His purpose.' I not only believed that I was
called; I believed that I was called according to God's purpose. I
believed in my heart from a young age that I had been called to
do something that only I could do. At the close of every day, I
would quote Romans 8:31—'If God is for us, who can be against
us?'

"Today, church, it is time for us to mature in Christ and know
that everything God has called us to do in this community, we
can accomplish. Yes, my calling demanded time away from the
church and time away from the family I love, but I rest in one
thing: God is faithful to complete that which He began in us."

I realized that the whole church was weeping. But theirs were
not tears of sorrow. They were tears of victory.

As the crowd dispersed, I shook a few hands and spoke to some of the kids. A few of the staff members remained along with my family. We went into my office, which had been decorated with banners and balloons. These small gestures that I had sometimes taken for granted in the past, I truly appreciated.

Walking toward my office, my mother grabbed my hand. With tears in her eyes, she embraced me. She stepped back and looked me in my eyes, holding both of my hands tightly. "John Jr.," she said, "you have done many things that have made me proud to be your mother, but I want you to know that seeing you take a stand and touch the lives of all of these young men and women makes my heart proud. Although your father has been dead for twenty years, I know he would have been proud of his baby boy. I want you to continue to speak these principles into the hearts of the young men and women in this community." She grabbed me by my ears and kissed me on my forehead, then was accompanied out of the church by one of our security guards.

As I turned to walk toward my office, I felt whole. It was as though I had been passed a mantle from my mother. It was a joy to know that my mother was pleased with the work that God had called me to do.

My wife asked the kids to sit in the conference room that was adjacent to my office. As soon as I closed the office door, she began to shed tears of joy. She hugged me like she never wanted me out of her sight again. Then she shared something with me that I will keep with me for the rest of my life. She told me that when I was first arrested, she felt I was being inconsiderate to the needs of my family. But during the long waiting process, God spoke to her clearly and gave her peace about the whole situation. She looked me in my eyes and assured me that everything we'd gone through was in the perfect will of God. "John," she said, "you will never know how many lives you touched by taking the stand you took."

She reached down, picked up her purse from the floor, and pulled out a small card. She handed it to me and asked me to read it.

The card read, *This trial opened my eyes to a lot of things. When it started, my intentions were to seek out the guilty and punish them to the fullness of the law. After hearing all the testimonies, I am convinced that God can and will change things. I want you and your husband to continue doing what you do. God has truly called you to be a blessing to the lost and the forgotten. Stand by your husband.* The card was signed, "Assistant District Attorney Tammy Reynolds."

Felice kissed me and opened the door to the conference room. I kissed all of my kids as they prepared to leave. This was normally my study night, so she and the kids left me to prepare for Sunday. I walked back into the sanctuary. It was empty now. I sat in the back row of our 1,500-seat auditorium and thanked God again for all that had transpired. It was about 11:40 P.M. and inside me was the burning desire to go out and tell somebody about Jesus.

I walked out by the rock that sat on the south end of our property. While I sat on the rock, two prostitutes and a crack user named Spoon walked by. The girls were arguing because Spoon wouldn't leave them alone. One of them said he was bad for business. He in turn told them he was their security guard. As they approached me, I imagined the first young lady leading our praise and worship. I imagined the second one speaking to our youth group, telling them how God had delivered her from prostitution. Lastly, I imagined Spoon teaching and preaching the Word of God and serving as codirector of our church's One Step program. (For all of those who think I'm crazy, don't forget what the blood of Jesus did for you.)

So there I was, sitting on that rock, believing God again to deliver someone who had been written off as hopeless by the rest of society. I guess you can imagine what I did next . . .

Pray for me.

DISCLAIMER

Although riveting and sometimes leaving you on the edge of your seat, the story that you have just read is **fiction**. The events in this book are fictitious; however, they are based on a compilation of actual events over the last twenty years and portray Pastor Kee's heart for ministry to those who are traditionally outside the reach of many churches.

While it tells the story of the twenty-two-song CD *Not Guilty, The Experience*, it is what Pastor John P. Kee describes "was clear from the motion pictures of my mind" and stimulated him to formulate *Not Guilty! The Script.*

We hope that this book stimulates you to go into the highways, byways, and the uttermost parts of the earth to let the hurting, the outcasts, and the downtrodden know that they are **NOT GUILTY!**

SHARE THE EXPERIENCE...
JOHN P. KEE MUSIC CATALOG

"Not Guilty ...the Experience"
0124 1-43139-2/3/4

"Mighty in the Spirit"
0124 1-43168-2/4

"Any Day"
0124 1-43117-2/4

"Strength"
0124 1-43108-2/3/4

"A Special Christmas Gift"
0124 1-43017-2/4

"Stand!"
0124 1-43014-2/3/4

"Show Up!"
0124 1-43010-2/3/4

"Colorblind"
0124 1-43009-2/4

"Lily in the Valley"
0124 1-43008-2/4

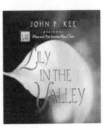

CASSETTES, CD'S & VIDEOS AVAILABLE